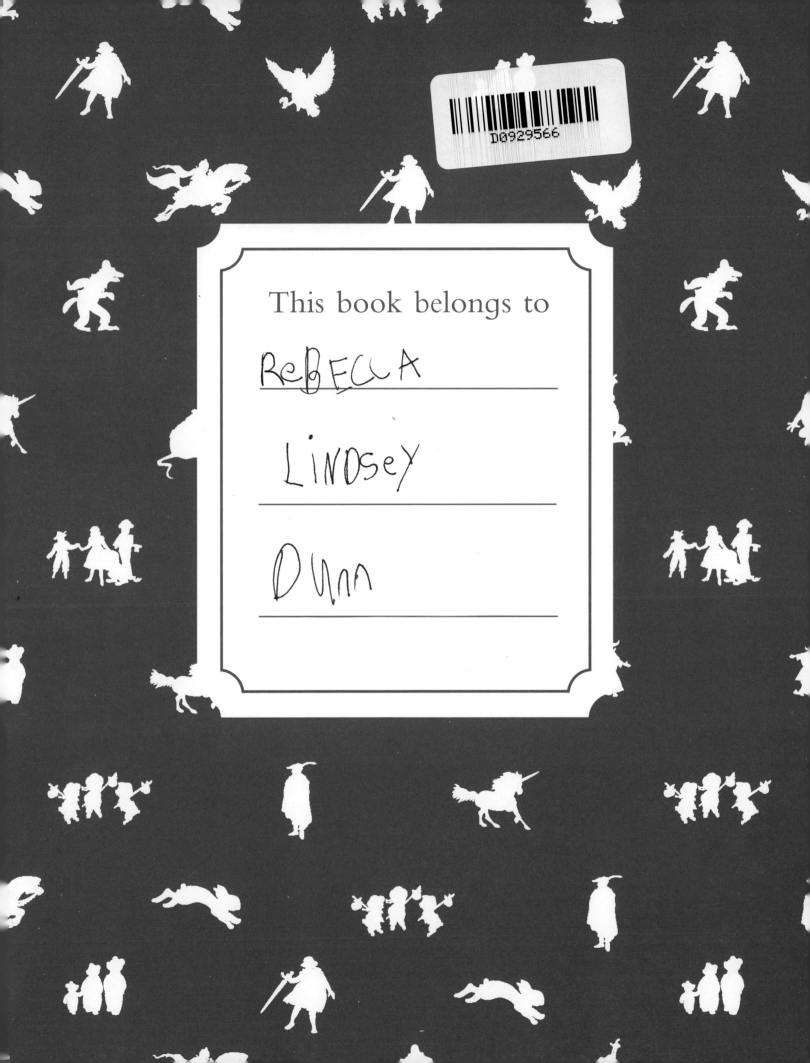

This book belongs to

REBECCA

LINDSEY

DUNN

MY Big Book OF BEDTIME STORIES

**This book was created by Zigzag Publishing,
an imprint of Quadrillion Publishing Ltd.,
Godalming, Surrey GU7 1XW.**

Edited by Helen Burnford and Kay Barnham
Design by Chris Leishman Design
Cover design by Triggerfish
Production by Karen Staff and Neil Randles
Translation from French by Chanterelle Translations
Color separation by Unifoto Ltd., South Africa
Printed and bound in India

Copyright © 1998 Quadrillion Publishing Ltd.
First published under the title Les Contes les Plus Célèbre
by Éditions Philippe Auzou, Paris
Illustrations © Éditions Philippe Auzou

This edition published in the U.S. in 1998 by
SMITHMARK Publishers, a division of U.S. Media Holdings, Inc.,
115 West 18th Street, New York,
NY 10011.

ISBN 0-7651-0695-7

SMITHMARK books are available
for bulk purchase for sales promotion
and premium use. For details write
or call the manager of
special sales,
SMITHMARK Publishers,
115th West 18th Street,
New York, NY 10011.

Ref. No. 8553

MY
Big Book
OF
BEDTIME
STORIES

SMITHMARK

Contents

Cinderella

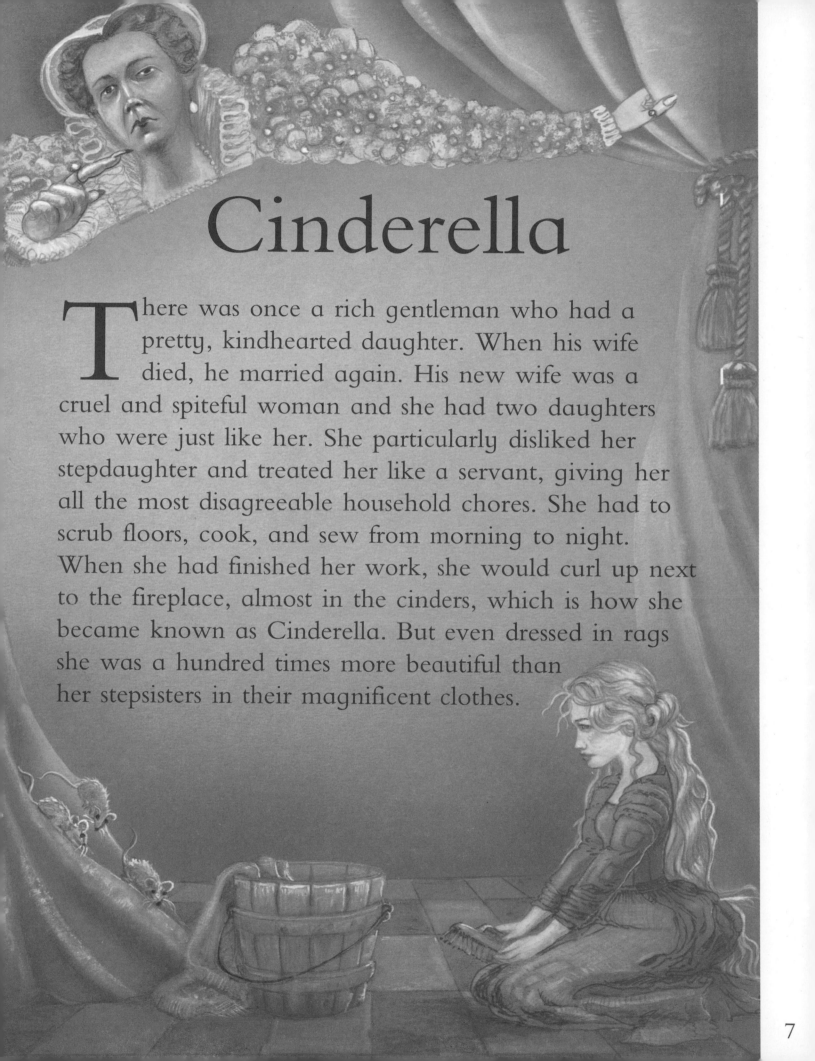

There was once a rich gentleman who had a pretty, kindhearted daughter. When his wife died, he married again. His new wife was a cruel and spiteful woman and she had two daughters who were just like her. She particularly disliked her stepdaughter and treated her like a servant, giving her all the most disagreeable household chores. She had to scrub floors, cook, and sew from morning to night. When she had finished her work, she would curl up next to the fireplace, almost in the cinders, which is how she became known as Cinderella. But even dressed in rags she was a hundred times more beautiful than her stepsisters in their magnificent clothes.

The king's son was giving a ball and invited all the noble people in the area. The two sisters were invited, but Cinderella was not. While she was helping them make their dresses they laughed at her and asked if she would like to go to the ball. But Cinderella knew she could not go dressed as she was, in her shabby, patched clothes, and she had nothing else to wear.

The day of the ball arrived and Cinderella kindly helped her stepsisters to dress. She polished their shoes, brushed their hair, and fastened their necklaces. As soon as the sisters had left for the ball, Cinderella burst into tears. "I would love to wear a beautiful dress and to dance all night," she whispered to herself.

Suddenly Cinderella heard a voice. She looked up and saw a dear old lady, dressed in a silver gown and carrying a sparkling magic wand.

"I am your Fairy Godmother," she smiled, "and if you would like to go to the ball, you must do as I say. Go into the garden and fetch me a large pumpkin. Then go and find me the mousetrap."

The Fairy Godmother tapped the pumpkin with her magic wand and it turned into a magnificent golden coach. Then she let the mice out of the trap and they were transformed into six prancing, dapple gray horses. A passing rat was instantly turned into a whiskery, old coachman. And for footmen, she found six lizards hidden behind a watering can. No sooner had she touched them with her magic wand than they climbed up behind the coach dressed in velvet uniforms.

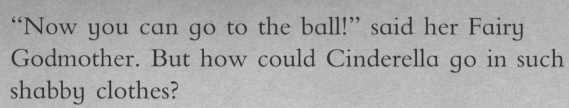

"Now you can go to the ball!" said her Fairy Godmother. But how could Cinderella go in such shabby clothes?

"Oh, I nearly forgot!" she chuckled as she touched Cinderella's rags with her wand. Instantly, they were changed into a beautiful ball gown embroidered with

gold and silver thread, and on her feet she wore a
pair of pretty glass slippers. Dressed like a princess,
Cinderella climbed happily into the coach.

"Now don't stay too late," her Fairy Godmother
warned, "on the stroke of midnight, my magic
will run out and all will be as it was!"

At the palace, Cinderella was greeted like a princess, but no one knew who she was. The prince only had eyes for her - the beautiful stranger who danced so gracefully - and he wouldn't dance with anyone else.

Cinderella was very sad to hear the clock strike quarter-to-twelve, but she hurried away from the glittering ballroom.

She ran down the stairs without even saying good bye to the prince. As she fled, she tripped, leaving behind one of her tiny glass slippers. And as the clock struck midnight, poor Cinderella stood outside the palace, dressed in her rags again. But the magic had not quite all gone . . . on her foot was the other glass slipper.

Shortly afterward, the prince announced that he would marry. But he would only marry the girl whose tiny glass slipper he had found on the stairs, even if he had to search far and wide for her.

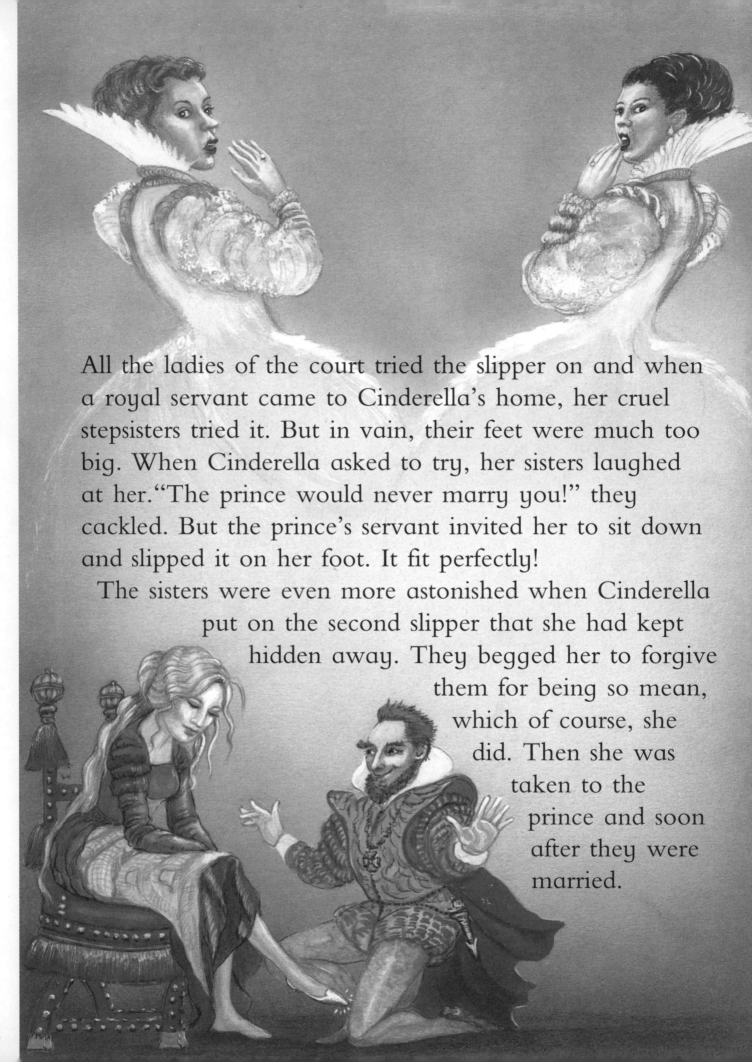

All the ladies of the court tried the slipper on and when a royal servant came to Cinderella's home, her cruel stepsisters tried it. But in vain, their feet were much too big. When Cinderella asked to try, her sisters laughed at her. "The prince would never marry you!" they cackled. But the prince's servant invited her to sit down and slipped it on her foot. It fit perfectly!

The sisters were even more astonished when Cinderella put on the second slipper that she had kept hidden away. They begged her to forgive them for being so mean, which of course, she did. Then she was taken to the prince and soon after they were married.

Sinbad the Sailor

Everyone calls me Sinbad the Sailor because I have spent nearly all my life at sea. This is the story of one of my adventures. When my father died, he left me a large fortune that I frittered away on extravagant parties and expensive clothes. Soon I had very little money left. Since I would rather have died than lived in poverty, I sold all I had and sailed for India with some merchants. One day, a storm rose and our ship was blown off course. The ship ran aground on a desert island, so beautiful it seemed like paradise. We split up to explore this wonderful place. After a while I fell asleep at the foot of a big tree, exhausted and hungry.

When I awoke, I searched in vain for my traveling companions, calling out to them at the top of my voice. But my only answer was the sound of the wind and the song of the birds. I ran to check where our ship was moored. All I saw was a tiny speck on the horizon. The ship was already far away and I had been abandoned on the island! I climbed to the top of a tall tree hoping to see a settlement on the island, but I could see nothing at all except a white mound, shaped like a large ball. I set off toward this strange object and when I reached it, found it was as smooth as marble. What can it be? I thought. There is no door and it seems hollow. Why don't I make a hole in it with a big stone? Suddenly the sky grew dark and I looked up and saw, just above me, a monstrous bird, snapping its enormous beak. The monster swooped down without noticing me, landed on the white object and flapped its wings.

Suddenly, I remembered. The sailors on

on board the ship had told me of a giant bird they called the roc, which was said to feed on snakes. So their incredible tale was true!

I must leave this island at all costs, I thought, and the roc can help me even without knowing it!

I undid my belt and knotted it around one of the bird's huge feet. I tied the other end to my wrist and waited. Soon the bird flapped its wings and took off into the sky, taking me with it! I trembled with fear. We were soaring so high that the island below looked like a tiny speck. After a while, the roc drew near to a small stretch of land surrounded by water. It seemed to be another island, bigger than the one we had just left. As soon as the bird landed I undid my belt and jumped down.

The bird did not see me because it was
staring at a fearsome snake that was threatening it,
displaying its forked tongue. The fight between the two
beasts was merciless. In the end, the roc tore the snake
to pieces before flying off. I shouted for joy, but my
happiness was short-lived for the island was nothing but
an enormous nest of snakes and the whole valley echoed
with their horrible hissing. I wondered despairingly
which was worse, to be pecked to death by an
enormous bird or swallowed by a monstrous serpent? I
had to find a hiding place to escape from the snakes.
Noticing a cave nearby, between two rocks, I crawled
in and waited for nightfall.

I was exploring my hiding place, which was lit by the sun's rays, when suddenly, I was dazzled by thousands of multicolored lights. I held out a hand and touched the stones that were scattered over the ground, and saw with amazement that they were precious diamonds! I sat there dazed, holding the treasure in my hands. The serpents' hissing seemed to have stopped, so I glanced outside.

Pieces of meat were falling from the sky. There were chops and enormous chunks of beef and mutton. You are going mad, Sinbad, I said to myself, thinking it was all a bad dream. Soon I saw a flight of enormous eagles swoop down onto the meat and fly off with it. It's as if someone is feeding them, I thought. This could provide me with another clever means of escape.

Cautiously, I left my hiding place. The snakes had slithered off as the eagles arrived. I took a piece of beef, attached it to my back and lay face down on the ground. I had been careful to fill my pockets first with precious jewels from the cave. If I survived, I intended to be rich!

Soon after, I heard a great rush of wings above me and an overpowering force lifted me up into the sky. The eagle, gripping the meat in its talons, with me hidden underneath, flew over the valley until it came to the rocky summit where it had built its nest. I was about to escape, when I heard shouts coming from below. Alarmed by the noise, the eagle flew off leaving the chunk of meat behind. I stood up and looking down, saw a small group of men, armed with sticks.

"Here I am, safe and sound," I shouted, jumping down from the nest. "Who are you?" asked the eldest of the men, who seemed to be their leader. "How did you get into the nest? Are you a merchant, like us?"

I told them the whole story. "It's a miracle you arrived today of all days," they exclaimed. "We only come here once every three years. We have thrown down all our meat and our harvest is finished." "Your harvest?" I said in surprise.

"The diamond harvest. The valley is so narrow that we can't reach the diamonds at the bottom, but we have found a good way of collecting them. We bring a cargo of meat with us and throw it in chunks to the bottom of the valley. The eagles spot the meat and carry it back to their nests and there are always diamonds stuck to the bottom of it. Then we only have to shout to frighten off the eagles before climbing up to their nests to collect the diamonds. Unfortunately, the biggest diamonds are still at the bottom of the valley. They fall off in flight because they are too heavy."

"For once you will not be disappointed," I told them, emptying my pockets of the jewels I had brought from the cave. That evening a great celebration was held and the next day we set off for home. I might have stayed quietly at home for the rest of my days, but I had acquired a taste for adventure and long voyages. I wanted to discover new countries. So I boarded a ship and sailed around the world, and another time, if you like, I'll tell you some more of my adventures . . .

Sleeping Beauty

There was once a king and queen. They were so happy to be celebrating the christening of their baby daughter that they invited the country's seven fairies to attend the party. Each fairy would give her a magic gift, and she would then possess every good quality. At the splendid christening banquet, each fairy was given a present of a set of magnificent solid gold knives and forks in a gold case, studded with precious jewels. But an eighth fairy appeared who had not been invited, because it was thought she was dead. The king and queen were unable to find an eighth gold case and the fairy flew into a terrible rage because she did not receive a present.

The fairies then bestowed their magic gifts on the baby princess. The first gave her beauty, the second, wit, and the third gave her grace. The fourth blessed her with the ability to dance, the fifth gave the gift of song, and the sixth, the gift of music. Then it was the old fairy's turn and she said, "The princess will prick her finger on a spindle and die!"

The guests gasped in horror. But the seventh fairy, who had been suspicious of the old fairy and had not yet bestowed her gift, stepped forward.

"I'm afraid I cannot undo the wicked curse completely," she said. "The princess will prick her finger on a spindle but will not die. She will sleep for a hundred years, after which a handsome prince will wake her with a kiss."

To try and prevent the wicked fairy's curse from coming true, the king forbade the possession and use of spindles, on pain of death.

"Throughout my kingdom, all spindles and spinning wheels must burn," he announced.

One day, when the princess was about sixteen years old, she was wandering from room to room in the enormous castle. She found herself at the top of a tower where an old woman, who had never heard of the ban, was spinning wool. The princess had never seen such a thing before and wondered if she might try spinning. It would be fun to try, she thought.

She turned the spindle, pricked her finger, and fainted. The old woman shouted for help and all the courtiers came running, but there was nothing they could do—the princess was fast asleep. The king hurried into the room and when he saw her he remembered the fairy's promise. He ordered that the princess should be carried to the most beautiful room in the palace. She was placed on a bed covered with gold and silver embroidery, dressed in her most magnificent clothes, and left to sleep. It was clear she was not dead, for she was still breathing softly. She looked as beautiful as an angel.

The good fairy who had saved her was sent for. Anxious that the princess should not feel lonely when she awoke, she touched everyone except the king and queen with her magic wand and they immediately fell into a deep sleep. Pages, ladies-in-waiting, servants, cooks, lords, footmen, and musicians all fell asleep, curled up, seated or lying down, with kindly smiles on their faces. The king and queen kissed their daughter good-bye and within a few moments, huge thorny brambles, tangled creepers, thick bushes, and trees had sprung up around the castle, making it impossible to reach.

A hundred years passed and one day a handsome prince was hunting nearby with his servants. He was curious to know who owned the strange castle whose towers could be seen above the thick forest. But no one could tell him. Some said it was certainly the home of witches, others thought a wicked ogre lived there. Then a very old man who lived in the wood approached the prince and said,

"My grandfather used to say, that in the most magnificent room in the castle lies a beautiful princess. She was cursed by a wicked fairy and has been asleep for a hundred years. Only a prince's kiss can wake her."

The prince's only thought was to reach the princess. But how was he to cross the wall of thorny brambles and creepers?

However, as he rode nearer, the brambles and trees
slowly drew apart to let him through, then suddenly
closed behind him, leaving his men on the other side.

He found himself alone in a strange and silent world,
listening to the barking of his dogs trapped on the other
side of the thicket. Not a single leaf rustled on the trees.
All around the castle, men, women, and animals were
sleeping. After stepping over the sleeping guards and
crossing many rooms, he discovered the princess who
looked about sixteen years old.

Her remarkable beauty and radiance won his heart and he leaned over and kissed her.

She immediately awoke.

"Are you my prince?" she asked.

The spell was broken and everyone in the palace woke up. The deathly silence was ended and a joyful commotion was heard all over the castle. Everyone ran around talking and laughing at once. The musicians began to play and great celebrations began.

Gulliver's Travels

Once upon a time in England, in the year 1712, there lived a young man named Gulliver. Gulliver loved to spend his days making long sea voyages. One day, he sailed away in a ship, called *The Antelope*, that was making for the South Seas. But the ship was wrecked in rough waters and there was only one survivor, Gulliver himself. After floating for days and nights, the young man managed to swim to a beach that seemed deserted. Exhausted, he fell into a deep sleep.

When Gulliver awoke he tried to stand up but discovered that his limbs were securely tied to the ground and that he was bound from head to toe.

"Help! Untie me!" shouted Gulliver. But he found, to his amazement, that he was being held prisoner by some tiny people who were barely six inches high. One of them, who was perched on his neck, stuck his tiny sword into Gulliver's nostril. It was so ticklish that Gulliver sneezed loudly. Terrified, all the little people scattered instantly.

After a few moments, the less timid among them approached Gulliver again and rested their ladders against his side. Soon, a multitude of little men holding

baskets filled to the brim with food, started to march toward his mouth. The emperor, who had himself been hoisted onto the end of Gulliver's leg, made his way toward Gulliver's mouth, followed by a dozen men. Once he had arrived, the emperor stood very close to Gulliver's face and announced,

"We greet you, oh Mountain Man, welcome to the country of the Lilliputians. We will treat you with great respect here, but be aware that you have plunged us into terrible trouble, for your appetite could ruin our country. We have held a council. Some of us talked of leaving you to die of starvation, or of piercing your face and hands with poisoned arrows, but your body, while

33

decomposing, would undoubtedly spread disease and a foul stench throughout the empire. We therefore propose the following. Help us to end the war that has been raging for thirty-six moons with the people of Blefuscu and we will give you back your freedom."

"But what started this war?" asked Gulliver.

"Well, everybody knows that to eat a boiled egg you have to crack the shell at the big end of the egg. It so happened that my great-grandfather, when he was a child, wanted to eat an egg. But by cracking the shell in the traditional way, he cut the tip of his finger. As a result, the emperor published a document ordering all his subjects, on pain of serious punishment, to crack their eggs at the little end. This law was so unpopular that it sparked riots, one of which meant an emperor lost his crown and another his life. The losses are estimated at eleven thousand men, who preferred to die rather than obey the law and crack their eggs at the little end. The Blefuscans took advantage of these uprisings to invade our country and kidnap half our population. Ever since, a bloody war has raged between the two empires. Today, the Blefuscans are preparing to invade our shores. This is why I place all my trust in you and in your courage."

The emperor's men untied Gulliver and took him to an ancient temple, believed to be the largest in the country. There, the "Mountain Man" was once again tied down with eighty-one chains, as heavy as the chains that in Europe are used as the bracelets for ladies' wristwatches. They were held in place on the left leg by thirty-six locks. All night, Gulliver tried to work out a plan to defeat the Blefuscan's navy. By morning, he had decided what to do.

The following day at dawn, he headed toward the northeast coast, which lay across from the shores of Blefuscu, and there, lying flat on his stomach, he took out his telescope to watch the enemy ships approaching. There were more than fifty miniature warships and many more troop transporter ships. Back in Lilliput, Gulliver gave orders to bring him very strong cables and metal bars. The cables were thin threads, and the bars were as long and as thick as the knitting needles. He bent the bars to make them into hooks and tied them to the cables before returning to the coast. He then waded into the water, which only came up to his chest, and moved quickly toward the enemy. On seeing him, the Blefuscans were so frightened that they all locked themselves in their tiny ships' cabins. Gulliver then took out the bars and cables, placed a hook at the prow of each ship and tied all the cables together in a knot. Then he grabbed the knot, and without any effort whatsoever, he dragged the fifty largest warships back to port.

The Blefuscans, who watched the scene from their shore, were rooted to the spot in astonishment. When they saw the fleet of ships being dragged away by

Gulliver they cried out in distress and despair. But Gulliver calmly made his way back to the port of Lilliput.

"Hurrah! Hurrah!" shouted the people of Lilliput, when they saw the "Mountain Man." The emperor greeted him on the beach and gave him the title of Nardac, which was the highest title of nobility.

37

About three weeks after this amazing event, a solemn group of politicians arrived from Blefuscu to seek peace. Great festivities were organized. Gulliver did not go to them however. Having recovered his freedom, he had built himself a boat and set off for home. To this day, a statue of Gulliver the hero, the "Mountain Man," towers over the central square in Lilliput.

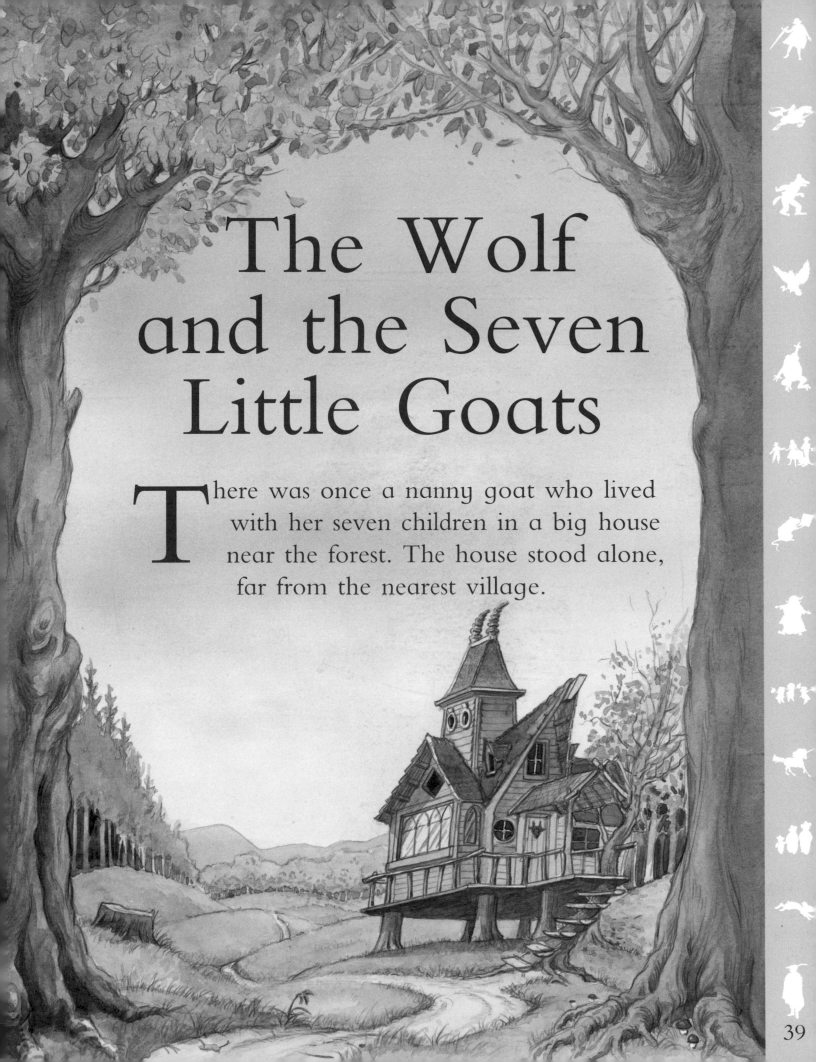

The Wolf and the Seven Little Goats

There was once a nanny goat who lived with her seven children in a big house near the forest. The house stood alone, far from the nearest village.

One day, the nanny goat said to her children,
"I must go shopping in the village to buy some more
food. Be good and stay indoors, and don't open the
door to anyone until I get back. A wicked wolf lives in
the forest and if you let him in, he'll eat you all up!"
The little goats promised to be good, and the nanny
goat took her basket and went out, closing the door
behind her.

But the wolf, who was hiding in the
forest, saw that the little goats
were alone and said to
himself, Yum, yum, seven
plump little goats! What
a good lunch I shall
have, to be sure!

Then he knocked at
the door and said in his
gruff voice, "It's
Mommy, let me in!"
But the little goats
replied,
"You're not our
mother. Our mother has a soft, gentle voice, and you
have a horrid, gruff voice. We know you're the wolf.
Go away!"

So the wolf hurried to the grocer's shop in the village and stole a pot of honey. He ate it all up and ran back to the little goats' house and knocked on the door, saying in a soft, gentle, but slightly sticky voice, "It's Mommy here. Let me in!"

But the little goats could see the wolf's paw against the window pane and answered, "You're not our mother. Our mother has a pretty white foot. Yours is black and ugly. We know you're the wolf so go away!"

So the wolf ran to the village again and went to the baker's where he stole some flour. He covered his foot in it and went straight back and knocked on the little goats' door. "It's Mommy here, let me in!" he said. And since he now had a soft, gentle voice and a white foot,

the little goats opened the door. When they saw it was
the wolf they shrieked with terror and ran away
to try and hide.
The first hid under the bed, the second under the table,
the third behind the curtains, the fourth in the grandfather
clock, the fifth in the bathtub, the sixth behind the door,
and the seventh under a chest of drawers. But the wolf
found them and ate them up, one after the other.

All except the
one who was hidden in the grandfather clock.

A little later, the nanny goat came home with her shopping. When she saw the door open and the house all topsy-turvy she cried,
"Whatever has been going on? Little goats, where are you? Answer me at once!"
The little goat who was hidden in the grandfather clock came out and told her what had happened.
"Don't worry," said his mother. "I saw the wolf sleeping near the river. We'll go and rescue your brothers and sisters. Run and fetch my sewing basket, my scissors, some stout thread, and a needle."

The little goat hurried off
to fetch them. Then
the nanny goat and the
little goat set off for
the riverbank.

They found the greedy
wolf lying by the river in the
sunshine. As he snored
peacefully, the nanny goat
careful snipped open his stomach
with her scissors. Out jumped
the six little goats!

"Run and collect some rocks
from the river," whispered
the nanny goat, and they
watched quietly as she
popped them into the
wolf's empty stomach. Then
she sewed up the wolf's
tummy and left him there,
fast asleep.

45

When the wolf awoke, he felt very thirsty.
I shouldn't have eaten all those little goats at once, he
thought and went to drink from the river. But his
stomach was so heavy that he could hardly walk and he
staggered to the water's edge. As he bent over to drink,
the weight of the stones pulled the wolf
into the water and down, down
to the riverbed. And no
one saw that
greedy wolf
ever again!

Snow White

There once was a good queen who pricked her finger on a needle. It was snowing and when she saw the drop of blood fall onto the white snow she thought she would like to have a little girl with lips as red as blood, skin as white as snow and eyes as black as ebony. Soon her wish was granted and she named her little baby Snow White.

But shortly afterward the good and gentle queen died and the king married again. His second wife was very beautiful but extremely vain. She was always looking in her mirror and asking, "Mirror, mirror on the wall, who is the fairest of them all?" The mirror could not lie and would answer,

"You, my queen, are the fairest of them all." But one day the mirror answered,

"You, my queen are fair, it's true, but Snow White is fairer now than you!"

The queen was overcome with hatred and ordered a hunter to kill Snow White, cut out her heart, and bring it back to her. The hunter took the child into the woods, but moved by her innocence and beauty, found himself unable to kill her. He told her,

"Run away! Run as far as possible without stopping, and don't come home." Then he killed a deer and took its heart to the queen who, suspecting nothing, believed it to be Snow White's.

In the forest, poor Snow White did not stop running until dusk fell when, trembling with fear, hunger, and cold, she noticed a light coming from a little house. She went up to the door and knocked, but there was no answer. She pushed open the door and went in. Inside, everything was in miniature, but clean and neat. There were seven little chairs and a table set with seven little knives and seven little forks. There were seven little tumblers and Snow White drank from each in turn, because she was so thirsty from running. There were seven little plates piled with food and she tasted some from each plate. Then she took a bite from each of the seven slices of bread. She was so hungry! Lastly, there

were seven little beds with white sheets on them and she lay down to sleep in the seventh.

The dwarfs who lived in the cottage came home after dark. When they saw that someone had eaten their supper, drunk from their tumblers, and was asleep in one of their beds, they were very surprised indeed. But they did not wake Snow White. The next day, when she told them her story, they asked her to stay and help them with the cooking and housework, safe from the wicked queen. She agreed and they were overjoyed. Before leaving for work, the dwarfs told her that on no account should she open the door to anyone.

The wicked queen, who was also a witch, consulted her mirror once more.

"Mirror, mirror on the wall, who is the fairest of them all?" She was very surprised to hear what it had to tell her. "You, oh queen, are fair, it's true, but Snow White is far fairer than you."

"How can this be? Snow White is dead," demanded the wicked queen. And the magic mirror told her,

"Snow White is alive and well. She lives deep in the forest with seven little dwarfs."
This time the wicked queen decided to kill Snow White herself. She put some poison into a beautiful red apple, and disguised as a peddler, visited the house of

the seven dwarfs. Snow
White would not come out of
the house, but when the old peddler held
a juicy apple up to the window, she could
not resist and took it. No sooner had the first bite passed
her lips than she fell down as though dead. The wicked
queen ran away laughing.

When the seven dwarfs came back from work, they
found Snow White lying on the floor, in a deep sleep.
They tried everything they could think of to revive her,
but it was no use. They cried over her for three days,
but since she was still so beautiful and rosy-cheeked,
they could not bear to bury her. They laid her in a
glass coffin, which they carried up the hill into the
sunlight. Night and day they took turns to watch over
her while the others went off to work.

One day, a prince who was passing by, stopped at the little house to ask for water. Seeing Snow White in her glass coffin, he was so struck by her beauty that he fell in love with her. He opened the glass coffin and took her in his arms. As he did this, the piece of poisoned apple fell from her mouth, and her eyes opened.

She saw the handsome prince and fell in love with him immediately. Snow White thanked her dear friends, the seven dwarfs, for taking care of her, and the prince took her to his kingdom where they were married and lived happily ever after.

The Three Little Pigs

Once upon a time there were three little pigs who went out into the world to seek their fortunes. The first little pig met a farmer who was carrying a large bundle of straw on his back.

"Please give me some of your straw to build a little house," he asked. The farmer agreed and the little pig built himself a pretty little straw house.

Some days later he heard a knock at the door. It was a wolf.

"Little pig, little pig, let me come in," he shouted.

"No! Not by the hair on my chinny-chin-chin," answered the little pig.

"Then I'll huff and I'll puff and I'll blow your house down," said the wolf.

And he huffed and he puffed so hard that the little straw house was blown away. Then he seized the little pig and ate him up in just one bite!

The second little pig met a man who was carrying a bundle of sticks on his back

"Please give me some of your sticks to build a little house," said the pig.

The man agreed and the little pig built himself a pretty little stick house. Some days later the wolf came by.

"Little pig, little pig, let me come in," he shouted.

"No! Not by the hair on my chinny-chin-chin," answered the little pig.

"Then I'll huff and I'll puff and I'll blow your house down," said the wolf. And he huffed and he puffed so hard that the pretty little rush house was blown away. Then he seized the little pig, popped him in his mouth, and swallowed him whole.

The third little pig met a man who was pushing a wheelbarrow full of red bricks. "Please give me some of your bricks to build a little house," said the pig. The man agreed and the third little pig built himself a little red brick house and planted roses by the door.

Some days later the wolf came by and knocked on the door. "Little pig, little pig, let me come in," he shouted.

"No! Not by the hair on my chinny-chin-chin," answered the little pig. "Then I'll huff and I'll puff and I'll blow your house down," said the wolf and he filled his lungs and huffed and puffed as hard as he could. But the house didn't move an inch.

The wolf was surprised and very cross. But then he had an idea.

"Little pig," he said kindly. "I know of a wonderful turnip field. Shall I tell you where it is?"

"Oh, yes please," said the little pig.

"It's right next to the carpenter's house. If you get up early tomorrow morning, we can go together and get a big bunch of turnips for dinner."

"What a good idea! What time will you call for me?" asked the little pig.

"At six o'clock in the morning, if that is convenient," replied the wolf, very politely.

But the next morning, the little pig got up at five o'clock and went to the turnip field by himself. He filled his basket with turnips and went happily home.

At exactly six o'clock, the wolf called at the little pig's house. "Are you ready?" he said.

"More than ready," replied the little pig. "I've already been to fetch some turnips for my dinner!"

The wolf was furious, but said nothing. "This little pig will soon be inside my stomach," he thought.

He said pleasantly, "Little pig, I know a place where there is an apple tree laden with apples."

"Please tell me where it is," said the little pig.

"In the baker's garden. Why don't you get up at five o'clock tomorrow and we'll go together?"

The next morning the little pig jumped out of bed before four o'clock had even struck. He hurried to the baker's garden but he had forgotten that it was so far away and that he would have to climb the apple tree. He had just reached the top when he saw the wolf.

"Well, well, little pig. I see you didn't wait for me to eat the apples. I hope they taste nice!"

"Delicious," replied the pig, "and here's a big juicy one I picked just for you." And he threw the apple as far as he could.

The wolf ran after it and while he was searching for it in the grass the little pig had time to climb down and run home. But the wolf would not give up, and the next day he called on the little pig again.

"I'm going to the fair this afternoon. Would you like to come with me?" he asked.

"With pleasure," said the little pig. "What time will you call for me?"

"At three o'clock sharp," replied the wolf.

The little pig went to the fair alone, well ahead of the wolf. He bought a wooden barrel, then set off for home. On the way, he saw the wolf coming to meet him! His only chance of escape was to hide inside the barrel, but while he was getting in, it started rolling down the hill straight toward the wolf. The wolf gave a frightened yelp and ran away as fast as his legs would carry him.

The next day the wolf came to the little pig's house, and told him about the terrible fright he had had. A huge wooden barrel had rolled straight toward him and nearly killed him! The little pig roared with laughter and said,

"You'll never guess who was inside the barrel. I went to the fair alone and bought a barrel. When I saw you, I hid inside the barrel and rolled toward you!" This was the last straw for the wolf who decided to finish off the little pig for once and for all.

"Just wait," he said under his breath. "I'm going to slide down the chimney and eat this little pig up."

But the little pig heard him on the roof and placed an enormous cooking pot, full of boiling water, on the fire. Just as the wolf was sliding down the chimney, he lifted the lid off the pot and the wolf fell in, head first. The little pig quickly put the lid back on and the wolf was cooked. And since that day, the little pig has lived safely and happily in his little red brick house.

The Frog Prince

Once upon a time there was a king whose daughters were all extremely beautiful. The king's castle stood near a thick, dark forest where, under an old lime tree in the forest, a clear, bubbling spring flowed. When the weather was very hot, the youngest princess would go and sit by the spring. To amuse herself, she would throw a golden ball in the air and catch it again. This was her favorite game. One day, the golden ball bounced away from her and fell into the waters of the spring.

The princess
began to cry.
Between her sobs, she
heard a voice saying,
"What is the matter, beautiful
princess, why are you crying as if your heart would
break?" The young girl looked around and saw an ugly
frog, sitting with just its head poking out of the water.

"Oh! it's you," she sobbed. "My golden ball has fallen in
the water. What shall I do?"

"Don't cry," replied the frog. "I can help you.

But what will you give me if I bring you back your toy?"

"Anything you want, dear frog! My dresses, my pearls, my
jewelry, even my golden crown."

The frog replied, "I don't want your dresses, your pearls, your jewelry, or even your golden crown. Just let me be your dearest friend. I should like to sit next to you at table, eat out of your golden plate, drink from your glass, and sleep in your little bed. If you promise me all that, I shall dive deep into the water and bring you back your golden ball."

"I'll promise anything you like. Go and look for it quickly," she said.

But really, she was thinking to herself, The poor frog has lost his head. How could someone who spends all his time in a pond croaking with other frogs, believe he was suitable company for a princess like me? He would make a very boring friend.

Content with the princess's promise, the frog swam off and reappeared on the surface of the water, holding the golden ball in his wide mouth. He threw it on the grass, and the princess, who was overjoyed at finding her toy again, picked it up and ran off. "Wait for me!" cried the frog. "I can't run as fast as you can!"

But the princess paid no attention to him. She went home to her father's palace and soon forgot all about the ugly frog.

But the next day, as she sat having dinner with the king and her sisters, there was a loud flop-flopping... flippy-flap... noise, like something wet climbing the grand marble staircase. When it reached the top, the thing knocked at the door and cried out, "Youngest child of the king, open the door!"

The princess ran to see who was outside. When she opened the door, she saw the frog. She slammed the door in his face and went back to her chair, where she sat trembling. The king noticed that his daughter was extremely upset about something, and he asked her,

"Why are you afraid, my child? Was there a giant at the door who was trying to kidnap you?"

"No, father," replied the princess. "It was not a giant, it was a hideous frog."

"What on earth does he want with you?" asked the king in astonishment.

"Oh dear, father!" moaned the princess, "yesterday I went to play in the forest beside the spring and my golden ball fell in the water. I was crying so bitterly that the frog dived in to fetch it, but he made me promise to treat him as a playmate."

They heard the frog knock at the door for the second time. The frog called out loudly,

"Youngest daughter of the king, open the door! Have you already forgotten the promise you made?"

The king then spoke resolutely, "Daughter, you must keep your promises. Let the frog come inside."

So the princess opened the door and the frog followed her to the table, and said to her, "Pick me up so that I can sit next to you." The princess hesitated.

"Do as the frog tells you," said her father. The frog had hardly sat down on the chair when he leaped onto the table. "Move your little gold plate closer and we shall eat off it together!" The princess did as he asked but very much against her will. The frog ate heartily, but the princess could hardly swallow a morsel.

"I have eaten so much that I'm feeling rather sleepy," said the ugly frog.

"Take me to your little room, it is time for us to go to sleep." The princess began to cry. She was frightened of the ugly frog. His skin was so cold and clammy and he wanted to sleep with her in her nice, cozy little bed!

But the king responded angrily. "My daughter, you should never despise anyone who helped you when you were in trouble."

So she picked up the frog with two fingers, took him up to

her bedroom. As soon as the princess had climbed into bed, the frog crept over to her and whispered, "Take me into your bed or I'll tell your father!" The princess's face reddened with rage. She picked up the frog and threw him as hard as she could against the wall.

"Take that, you ugly frog!"

To her amazement, when he fell to the ground, he was no longer an ugly frog. He became a handsome prince, whose eyes were full of love and tenderness. He explained that a spell had been cast over him by a wicked witch and that she had released him from the terrible curse. The princess immediately fell in love with him. With the king's blessing, the prince married the princess and took her away to his kingdom the very next day.

The Ugly Duckling

It was summertime and the air was scented with newly mown hay. In the forest, among the tall trees, there stood a castle surrounded by a moat. Thick clumps of weeds grew at the foot of the castle walls. In this quiet spot, a duck had built a nest and was sitting on her eggs. She sat for a long time hoping that something would happen. Eventually, the eggs hatched, one by one.

"Tweet, tweet!" the tiny little ducklings cried as they broke out of their shells, their eyes wide with astonishment. The world was so big!

The duck carefully counted her ducklings, but the biggest egg remained unbroken. An elderly duck who was passing advised her to abandon this last egg, which might be a turkey egg. But the duck, who had waited for such a long time, decided to sit on it just a little longer.

Finally, the shell cracked and a large, gray, ugly ball of fluff emerged, looking nothing like the other ducklings. Never mind! thought the mother duck, as she watched over her ducklings.

The next day, the mother duck leaped into the waters of the moat. The ducklings dived in one after the other

behind her and bobbed along on the water.
Even the big, ugly, gray duckling joined in.
 So it can't be a turkey chick after all, it swims too well for
that! It really must belong to me, she thought.
 "Come along. Stay right behind me all of you, and beware
of the cat!" said the mother duck to her ducklings.
 "Hurry along now and don't forget to bend your necks and
bow to Old Lady Duck!" quacked the mother duck.
All the ducklings obeyed,
dipping their bills
down low.

The other ducks made fun of the big ugly duckling.
One duck even leaped on him and bit his neck.
"Leave him alone! He isn't doing any harm! He may
not be very handsome but he swims very well, and with
time his looks may change!" said the mother duck sadly.
The poor ugly duckling became a laughingstock. The
drakes, roosters, and hens bit and pecked at him and the
turkey fluffed out all his feathers and charged at him.
The ugly duckling did not know what to do with
    himself, and he became more and more sad.

Even his brothers and sisters made fun of him.

"I hope the cat gets you, you ugly thing!" they quacked. Even his mother said to him, "If only you would go away! You don't really belong with us."

So one evening, the duckling decided to leave and hopped away over the hedge.

Sad and exhausted, the ugly duckling spent the night on the marshes. Even the wild ducks who lived there made fun of him.

"Fly away home!" they quacked at him, "you don't belong here."

So he hid out of sight for three days. Then, two geese who were passing by said to him, "Listen, friend, it doesn't matter to us how you look. Why don't you fly away with us?"

75

But the duckling's wings had not grown enough and he couldn't fly. So the two geese flew away to join their other friends, and the little duckling was on his own again.

The fall leaves swirled in the icy wind and the poor ugly duckling shivered in the cold. As the sun began to set, a flight of large birds with long, waving necks appeared over the treetops. They were swans who were flying away for the winter. The duckling had never seen such beautiful white birds. They opened their powerful wings and flew higher and higher. Full of excitement, the ugly duckling stretched his neck to the sky to admire the beautiful sight. He let out a cry, which was so strange and piercing, he was frightened of it himself. He did not know the name of these marvelous birds, but he longed to be like them.

The winter was terribly cold and the hollow in which the duckling slept soon filled with snow. It was more and more difficult to find anything to eat beneath the thick ice on the lake. The poor, lonely duckling soon became very weak. One morning, a man saw him, lying on the ice. He picked him up and

took him home to his wife, who put him in front of the warm stove. The children wanted to play with the duckling, but he was frightened of them. So when the door was open, he flapped his little wings and ran out into the cold again.

One day, the sun began to warm the marshes. It was spring again. The duckling flapped his wings and to his great surprise, he could fly. He glided on his strong wings, into a beautiful garden.

Three white swans glided gracefully on the surface of a pond. If I fly over to them, he thought, they might hiss at me because I am so ugly! But as he flew over, he could see his reflection in the surface of the water. He saw that he was no longer an ugly gray duckling, he had turned into a beautiful swan! So he landed gracefully on the pond and joined the other, beautiful, white swans.

Hansel and Gretel

Once upon a time a poor woodcutter lived in the forest with his family. His wife was old and cruel, but he loved his two children, Hansel and Gretel, dearly. The woodcutter worked hard, but there was never enough food in the house. One day, the woodcutter's wife announced, "Tomorrow, we are going to take the children deep into the forest and leave them there." The woodcutter was horrified but his wife persuaded him that they must do this, or they would all starve. But Hansel, who had been kept awake by hunger, had heard everything that had been said. He got up, went outside, and gathered plenty of small white pebbles which he put in his pocket.

The next morning, the whole family went out into the forest. "Stay here," said the wife. "We are off to look for some wood and we'll come back very soon." But of course, they never came back. Fortunately, Hansel had sprinkled the white pebbles along the path. He took his little sister's hand and by nightfall the two children had found their way home.

The old wife was very angry when she saw the children on the doorstep. She said to the woodcutter,

"Tomorrow, we will go even deeper into the forest and then they will never be able to find their way back."

Once again, Hansel had heard everything, but when he tried the door it was locked. This time Hansel couldn't collect pebbles. The next morning, they all walked into the forest. Farther and farther they went and the woodcutter and his wife walked on far ahead. Hansel and Gretel were very hungry, but instead of eating the bread they had been given, Hansel had crumbled it and thrown it down on the path behind him.

"We will follow the crumbs and that is how we will find our way home," he told his sister. They were very tired, as they had walked so far, and they soon fell asleep on a mossy bank. When they woke up it was almost nighttime. The woodcutter and his wife had gone. But when the children tried to find their way home, the bread crumbs were nowhere to be seen! The birds had eaten them.

"Now we shall never find our way home!" cried Gretel. She was very sad and was about to burst into tears when, suddenly through the trees, the children spied a dear little house. The little house was built of gingerbread. The roof was made of delicious cookies and the shutters were candied sugar. The children were so hungry that they broke a piece of the roof off and ate it. While they were enjoying the delicious taste, an old lady came out, cackling to herself.

She was a wicked witch who liked nothing better than to cook and eat little children. She had seen Hansel and Gretel in the forest and had used her magic to create the little gingerbread house. But she pretended to be kind and invited the two children in to share her meal. Once dinner was over, they were so exhausted, the children fell asleep immediately. When they woke up, Hansel found himself shut in a cage and called to Gretel for help. It was then that Hansel and Gretel realized that the old woman was a witch!

"You will do the cleaning and cooking," the wicked witch ordered Gretel. "And when your brother is nice and fat, I'll eat him."

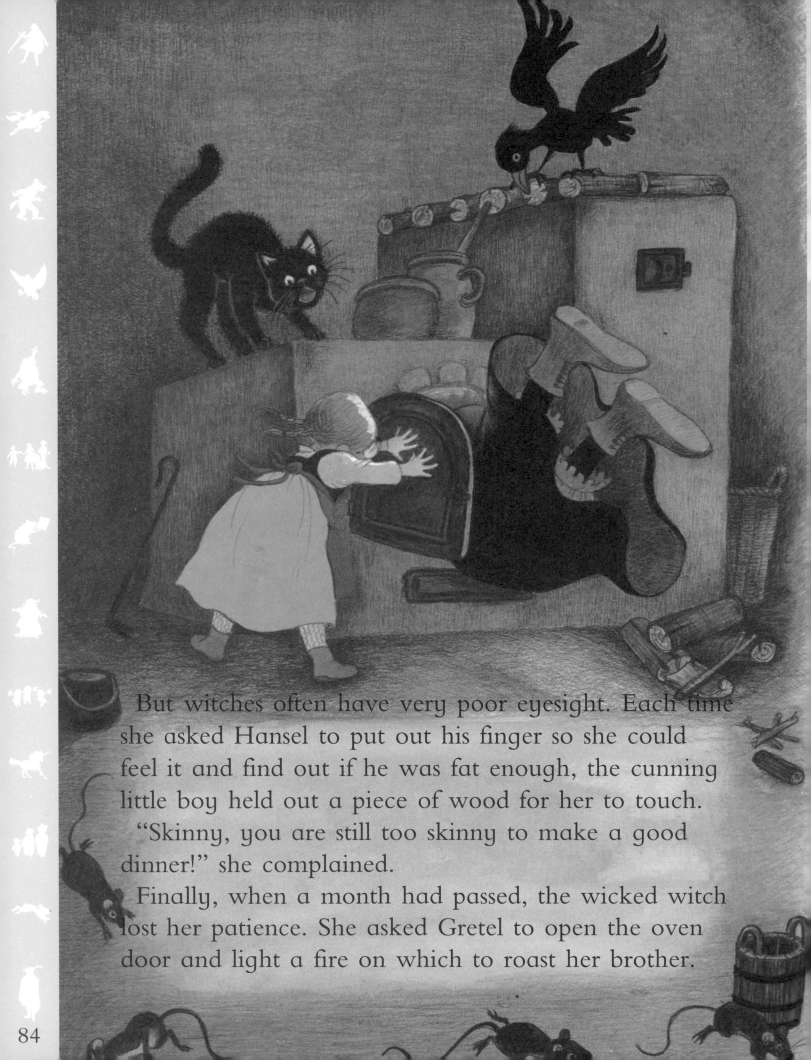

But witches often have very poor eyesight. Each time she asked Hansel to put out his finger so she could feel it and find out if he was fat enough, the cunning little boy held out a piece of wood for her to touch.

"Skinny, you are still too skinny to make a good dinner!" she complained.

Finally, when a month had passed, the wicked witch lost her patience. She asked Gretel to open the oven door and light a fire on which to roast her brother.

When the witch bent over to see whether the fire was hot enough, Gretel pushed her inside, shutting the door tightly behind her. The old woman shouted and shouted, but eventually she stopped. Gretel rushed over to free Hansel from the cage.

Inside the house, the children discovered a sack filled with gold, diamonds, and precious stones. "Now we can go home," the children cried joyfully.

Hansel and Gretel were soon on the path home. On their way, they discovered a magical lake where large white swans glided over the clear water. The two children would have to cross the lake in order to get home, but they could not swim because their pockets were so heavy with the treasures they had found.

"I have an idea!" exclaimed Gretel. "We can each sit on the back of a swan and they will carry us across to the opposite bank." So that is what the children did.

When they arrived home, the woodcutter wept with joy to be reunited with his dear little children. Since they had been gone, his cruel wife had died, leaving him all alone. Hansel, Gretel, and their father promised never to leave each other again. They lived happily ever after and were never short of anything.

The Emperor's Nightingale

Once upon a time there was a Chinese emperor who lived in the most magnificent palace in the world. His gardens, in which the most beautiful flowers bloomed, were enchanted and magical. There was a nightingale who had made a nest on one of the branches of a flowering tree. The bird's song was so glorious that everyone around stopped working just to listen to it. Visitors from every land flocked to the imperial city and all were amazed by the palace and the gardens. But when they heard the nightingale, they cried out for joy, "What a wonderful sound!"

Each told the other how delightful the bird song was, until the news even reached the ears of the emperor himself. The emperor flew into a rage.

"Who does this nightingale think he is?" demanded the old ruler angrily. "I do not know him. He is one of my subjects, he lives in my garden, and I have never heard him. Bring him to me and let him sing to me in person!" And he sent a servant to find the nightingale in its nest. Special preparations were made at the palace to receive the famous singer. The walls and floors gleamed in the light of a hundred thousand golden lanterns.

In the middle of the great hall in which the emperor received visitors, a golden twig had been placed on which the nightingale was to perch.

All eyes were fixed upon the little gray bird, who sang

so divinely that tears came to the emperor's eyes.

As the tears ran down the cheeks of the old man, the song of the nightingale grew sweeter and sweeter. His voice touched everyone's heart and he became a star. The whole town talked about the magical bird that had become the jewel of the kingdom.

Then one day, the emperor received a large parcel containing a mechanical nightingale. It was designed to imitate a real nightingale and was covered with diamonds, rubies, and sapphires. It was so beautiful and like the other nightingale, sang so well that everyone wanted to hear the two nightingales sing in concert. So they were made to sing together. But the duet sounded quite wrong, because the real nightingale sang from natural inspiration while the other followed its mechanical movement. So the artificial bird was made to sing alone. It was as popular as the real bird and was far more pleasing to the eye, because it sparkled with precious jewels.

It sang the same passage thirty-three times over without becoming in the least bit tired, and so pleased the crowd that they chased the real nightingale away. The real nightingale was banished from the city and the empire, and the artificial bird took the seat of honor on a little lacquered table beside the emperor's bed.

But one evening, when the mechanical bird was singing his heart out and the emperor was listening enraptured from his bed, there was a sudden "crack!" from inside the bird's body, then a "br-rr-oo-oo." All the gear wheels jammed and the music stopped abruptly. The wonderful mechanism had rusted. The mechanical bird would never sing again.

Five years later, the country was plunged into deepest gloom. The Chinese greatly loved their emperor, but he had fallen ill and it was said that he was about to die. A new emperor had already been elected and all the people had assembled in the great square to welcome him.

The old emperor lay pale and cold in his bed. He found it so hard to breathe, he felt as if people were tramping on his chest. As he opened his eyes, he saw Death. It had come to fetch him. The emperor was very frightened at the thought that his last hour had come.

Then suddenly from the window, a delightful song was heard. It was the little nightingale from the forest who sat trilling on a branch. It had learned of the emperor's illness and had come to cheer him up and to bring him hope. The little nightingale sang so beautifully and so sweetly that the emperor's terrible visions of death disappeared. As if by magic, the old man was cured and regained his strength immediately.

"Thank you, thank you, heavenly little bird," he exclaimed. "I once chased you away and yet your singing has chased away the evil spirits. How can I reward you?"

"You have already rewarded me," sang the nightingale.

"I brought tears to your eyes the first time I sang. For me, those are diamonds and I shall never forget them. Let me come and visit you whenever I can. I shall sing to you of the joyful and the sad, about good and evil, about all the things you know nothing about, because a little bird flies everywhere and sees everything. Only promise me one thing, do not tell anyone that you have a little bird who tells you everything. Believe me, it is for the best."

And the little nightingale flew away. A moment later, the courtiers and servants entered the room to see the dying emperor for the last time. They were astonished when the emperor sat up and wished them a hearty, "Good day!"

Puss in Boots

Once upon a time there was a miller who had three sons. When he died, all he left them was his mill, his donkey, and his cat. The treasures were soon shared out. The oldest son got the mill, the second-oldest took the donkey and all that was left for the youngest son was the cat.

"It's not fair!" he wailed. "What shall I do with this wretched cat?"

"Don't cry, master," said Puss. "All you have to do is sew a big sack for me and give me a pair of good, strong boots."

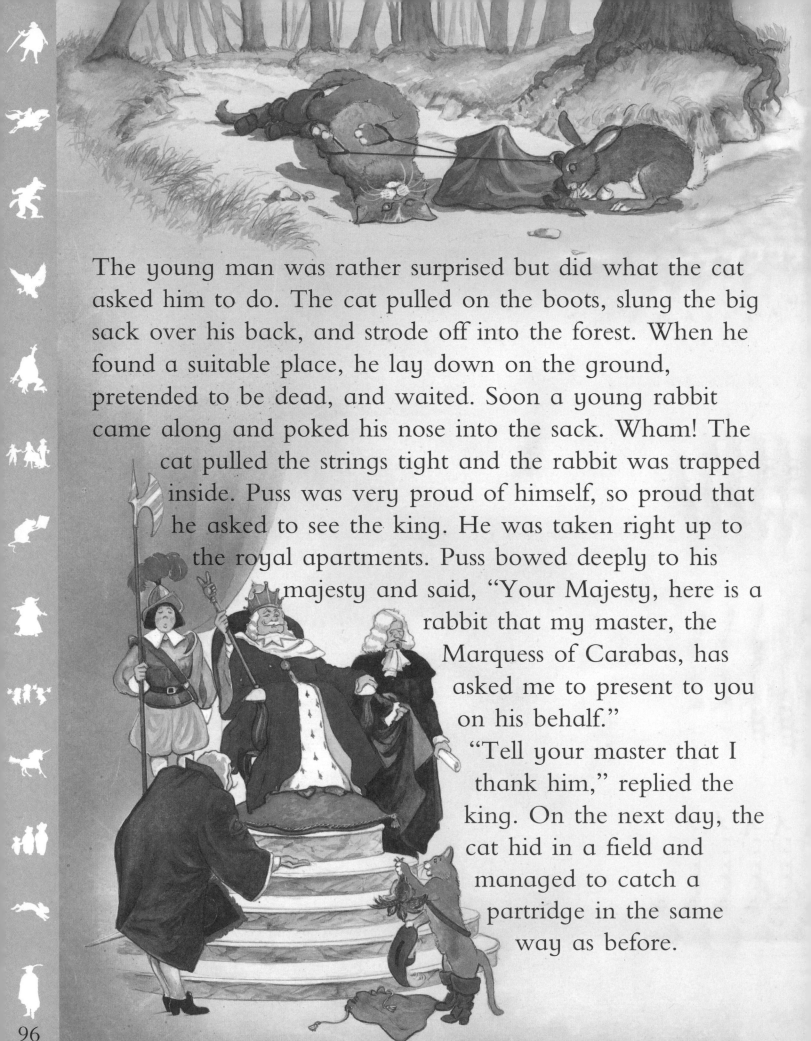

The young man was rather surprised but did what the cat asked him to do. The cat pulled on the boots, slung the big sack over his back, and strode off into the forest. When he found a suitable place, he lay down on the ground, pretended to be dead, and waited. Soon a young rabbit came along and poked his nose into the sack. Wham! The cat pulled the strings tight and the rabbit was trapped inside. Puss was very proud of himself, so proud that he asked to see the king. He was taken right up to the royal apartments. Puss bowed deeply to his majesty and said, "Your Majesty, here is a rabbit that my master, the Marquess of Carabas, has asked me to present to you on his behalf."

"Tell your master that I thank him," replied the king. On the next day, the cat hid in a field and managed to catch a partridge in the same way as before.

Once again, he went off to present the partridge to the king on behalf of his master. Every day, week after week, Puss continued to bring game to the king, and each time he did so, the king was delighted with the gift.

One day, Puss learned that the king was going for a drive by the river with his daughter, the most beautiful princess in the world. Puss said to his master, "If you do as I tell you, your fortune is made. All you have to do is bathe in the river

at the spot that I shall show you, and then let me do the rest."

The miller's youngest son did as his cat said, without knowing what Puss had in store for him. While he was bathing, the king passed by. Puss shouted as loudly as he could, "Help! Help! The Marquess of Carabas is drowning!" The king leaned out of the royal coach. He recognized the cat and ordered his guards to go and help the marquess.

While the marquess was being helped out of the water, Puss explained to the king that his master's clothes had been stolen while he was bathing. The king immediately ordered fresh clothing to be brought for the marquess to wear.

Now that he was dressed like a prince, the young miller's son looked extremely handsome. The princess, who was in the royal coach, found him very much to her liking. The marquess glanced at her several times, tenderly but respectfully, and she fell madly in love with him. The king asked the marquess to join him in the royal coach and accompany him and his daughter on their outing.

Puss ran ahead all along the way. When he came to some workers who were mowing a field, he said to them,

"Listen to me. Unless you tell the king that the field you are mowing belongs to the Marquess of Carabas, I'll make mincemeat out of you!"

As the king passed by, he asked the workers who owned the field they were mowing. They replied that it was owned by their master, the Marquess of Carabas. Puss had frightened them badly!

"What a handsome field you have there!" said the king to the pretend marquess.

"It brings in a lot of money every year," replied the miller's son.

Puss, who had continued to run ahead of the coach, met some men who were harvesting.

"Listen to me, unless you tell the king that all the wheat in this field belongs to the Marquess of Carabas, I'll make mincemeat of you!"

The king arrived a moment later and asked who owned all this beautiful, golden wheat.

"It belongs to the Marquess of Carabas!" said the harvesters.

The king was astonished at how rich the Marquess of Carabas was!

Finally, Puss reached a magnificent castle that was owned by a very rich ogre. The fact is that all the land that the king had passed through actually belonged to the ogre. Puss demanded to speak to him, saying he had not wanted to pass so close to the castle without paying his respects.

The ogre received him in as friendly a manner as an ogre can.

"I have been told," said Puss," that you can change yourself into the shape of all sorts of animals. A lion or an elephant, for instance."

"That's true," said the ogre proudly. And he immediately changed himself into a huge and terrible lion. Puss jumped out of the window

and ran off to hide on the roof. "I have also been told," continued the cat, once the ogre had returned to his normal shape, "that you can take on the appearance of tiny little animals too, a mouse, for example. But that seems to be impossible!"

"Impossible?" roared the ogre. "I'll show you!" And he changed into a little mouse who ran across the floor. Puss pounced on the mouse and swallowed him in one mouthful.

In the meantime, the king had reached the gate of the castle and wanted to go inside. The cat, hearing the sound of the coach, ran to the gate.

"Your majesty is most welcome at the castle of the Marquess of Carabas!" he declared proudly.

"How is it possible, marquess, that you own this castle as well?" cried the king. "I have never seen such a magnificent castle. Let us go inside and see it."

The miller's son offered his arm to the young princess, and they followed the king inside. A sumptuous feast awaited them in a beautifully decorated hall. The king was delighted and raised his glass to the marquess.

"Just say the word, marquess, and you shall marry my beautiful daughter." The marquess, bowing deeply, accepted the honor that the king had done him. And that very day, he married the beautiful princess.

Now that he had become a nobleman, Puss hardly ever chased mice again, except once in while, to amuse himself.

Goldilocks and the Three Bears

Once upon a time there was a little girl who had long golden hair, and for this reason she was known as Goldilocks. Goldilocks lived with her mother in a pretty little house at the edge of the forest. One day, she said to her mother, "I'm going for a walk, and I'll bring back a beautiful bunch of flowers that I'll pick especially for you."

103

"That would be nice, Goldilocks. But be careful not to go too far. You might get lost!" her mother warned. Goldilocks hugged her mother, hung her basket on her arm, and went off.

She began by picking some beautiful big white daisies. Then, a little farther on there were some blue cornflowers.

And farther still, there were glorious red poppies. As she ran from flower to flower, Goldilocks began to lose all sense of time.

She soon became tired and began to feel very hungry and thirsty. Fortunately, she saw a little house among the trees.

She looked through the keyhole, and as she couldn't see anyone inside, she pushed open the door and walked right in.

Inside there was a big table laid with three bowls full of honey and rice. It smelled delicious! There was a big bowl, a middle-sized bowl, and a little bowl. Around the table, there stood three chairs that looked very comfortable. There was a big armchair, a middle-sized chair, and a little chair. Goldilocks sat down in the big armchair, but it was too hard and she felt uncomfortable. She tried the middle-sized chair, but the cushion was too soft and she slid around on it.

So she sat down in the little chair, but she was too heavy; the legs broke under her and she fell on the floor!

Feeling very hungry, she decided to taste the rice and honey pudding. She took a spoonful from the big bowl, but it was too hot and she burned her tongue. She tried the middle-sized bowl but it was too lumpy.

Finally, she tasted the little tiny bowl. The pudding was absolutely delicious, and Goldilocks gobbled up every last drop!

As she was very tired, Goldilocks felt like having a little nap. She went upstairs to the bedroom where she found three beds. There was a big bed, a middle-sized bed, and a little bed. She tried the big bed, but it was too hard and rather uncomfortable. She tried the middle-sized bed, but the blankets were scratchy and she could not get to sleep.

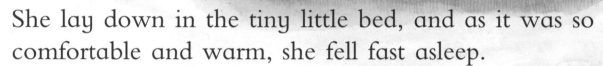

She lay down in the tiny little bed, and as it was so comfortable and warm, she fell fast asleep.

Meanwhile, the family of bears who lived in the house, arrived home after their walk. As soon as they opened the front door, they could smell that someone had been there and they began to search the room, sniffing everywhere.

"Someone has been sitting on my chair," exclaimed
Daddy Bear in his big, deep voice.

"Someone has touched my cushion," cried Mommy
Bear in her gentle voice.

"Look, someone has broken my chair!" said Baby Bear
in his squeaky little voice, and
he burst into tears.

Then the bears went over to the table.

"Someone has licked my spoon," growled Daddy Bear in his big, deep voice.

"Someone has touched my bowl," said Mummy Bear in her gentle voice.

"Look, someone has eaten up all my pudding, and there is nothing left!" cried Baby Bear, and tears rolled down his long nose.

Then the bears went upstairs. Daddy Bear sniffed and
growled in his deep voice,

"Someone has been lying on my pillow!"

"Someone has moved my blankets," said
Mommy Bear quietly.

"Look, look, there is a little girl asleep in my bed!"
shouted Baby Bear, in surprise.

When Goldilocks heard the voices, she woke up.
Seeing the three bears leaning over her, she was
very frightened.

She jumped quickly out of bed, leaped through the window, and ran off into the forest. She ran home as fast as her legs would carry her, without looking back once! And the bears never saw Goldilocks in the forest again.

Aladdin and the Magic Lamp

Once upon a time, faraway in the East, lived a young boy named Aladdin. He was very poor and spent his days, like many other children of his age, roaming the streets.

One afternoon, while Aladdin played in the town square with his friends, a mysterious stranger came up to him. The man wore splendid, silken robes. On his head sat a huge turban encrusted with a magnificent sapphire. He had a little pointed, black beard and his bright eyes fixed on Aladdin.

"Are you the son of Mustapha the tailor?" he asked. "My boy, would you like to earn a few rupees?"

"Oh! Yes, sir! I would do anything to have some money to take home!"

"Well, Aladdin, listen carefully."

"All you have to do is squeeze through a narrow hole and bring me back an old lamp."

Aladdin followed the stranger until they came to a place a long way from the town. They lifted a heavy marble slab and the young boy, who was slim and agile, slipped through the opening and followed a few steps that led down into the ground. The man removed a ring from his finger and held it out to Aladdin,

"Put this ring on your finger, it will protect you against all harm."

He did this and carried on down. At the bottom of the steps, Aladdin discovered a huge cave. There he found great chests and golden jars filled with jewels, and trees sagging under the weight of fruit made of diamonds, pearls, and opals. It was a treasure trove!

Aladdin stared in wonder until he heard a loud cry,

"The lamp, Aladdin, bring me the lamp!" Aladdin looked all around him and finally found an old oil lamp standing on a chest.

Why does the stranger want this worthless lamp when

the whole place was overflowing with riches? He must certainly be a magician, he thought to himself. Aladdin was worried, but he took the lamp and slowly climbed back up the steps.

"Give me the lamp," ordered the man, who was becoming impatient.

"Help me out," cried Aladdin.

"First give me the lamp!" shouted the stranger. But Aladdin went back down the steps without answering.

"All right then, stay down there, if you like it so much!" And in his rage, the man pushed the marble slab back over the hole!

Alone in the cave, Aladdin was terribly afraid. He sat in the darkness and wrung his cold hands in despair. The ring he still wore on his finger began to shine and suddenly an amazing figure appeared before him. His eyes gleamed beneath a large white turban, and his hands were crossed on his chest.

"I am the genie of the ring. Speak and I shall obey!" his voice boomed.

"I want to go home," wailed Aladdin.

No sooner had he spoken, Aladdin found himself with the lamp and the ring, back in his own home. He

told his mother his strange adventure. While she listened to him, she began to polish the old lamp to make it shine. As soon as she rubbed it, thick smoke began to pour out of the spout. From out of the smoke appeared another genie. This one was even more awesome than the first.

"I am the genie of the lamp. Speak and I shall obey!"

From that day on, Aladdin and his mother lacked for nothing. Whatever they wished for, the good genie of the lamp immediately granted.

As the years went by, Aladdin turned into a tall,

handsome young man. One morning he saw Badrulbudur, the sultan's daughter, in the marketplace and fell in love with her. The sultan was impressed by the young man's wealth and soon agreed to grant him the princess's hand in marriage.

After a lavish wedding ceremony, Aladdin and Badrulbudur went to live in a magnificent palace, which the genie had built.

One day, when the young princess was alone in the palace, a strange merchant stopped beneath her window.

"New lamps for old, new lamps for old," he cried. "Who wants to exchange their old lamp for a new one?"

Badrulbudur was unaware of Aladdin's secret and the existence of the genie. She found the old lamp and exchanged it with the merchant, who was none

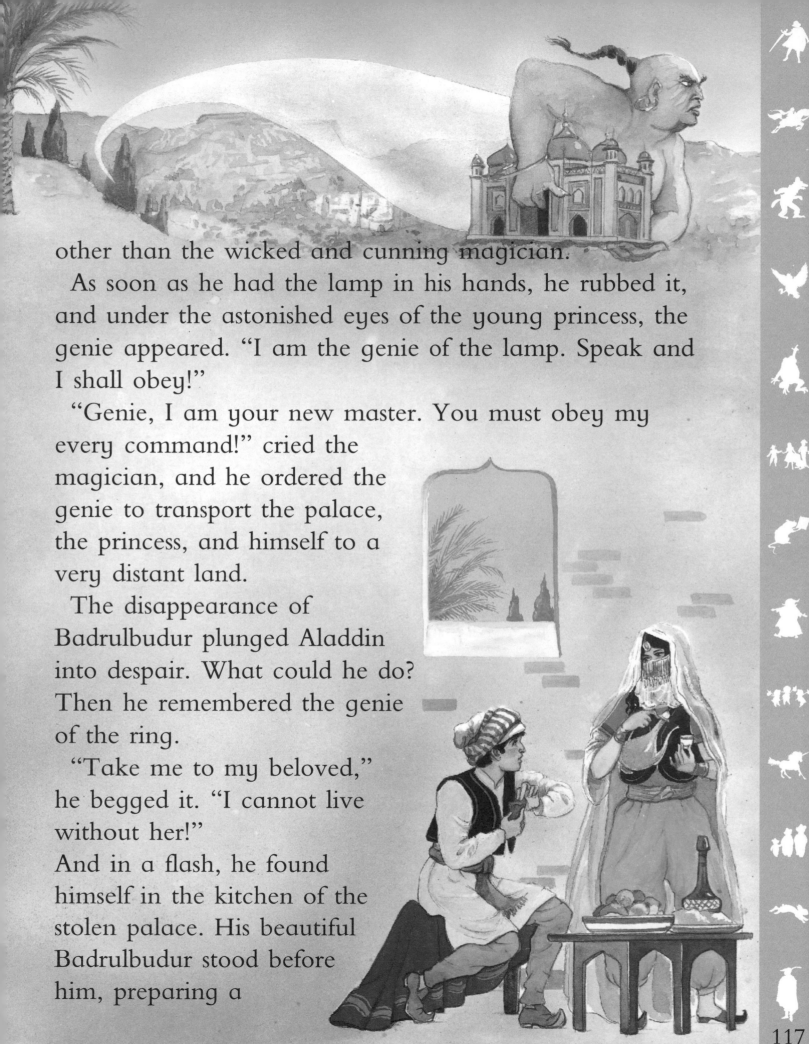

other than the wicked and cunning magician.

As soon as he had the lamp in his hands, he rubbed it, and under the astonished eyes of the young princess, the genie appeared. "I am the genie of the lamp. Speak and I shall obey!"

"Genie, I am your new master. You must obey my every command!" cried the magician, and he ordered the genie to transport the palace, the princess, and himself to a very distant land.

The disappearance of Badrulbudur plunged Aladdin into despair. What could he do? Then he remembered the genie of the ring.

"Take me to my beloved," he begged it. "I cannot live without her!" And in a flash, he found himself in the kitchen of the stolen palace. His beautiful Badrulbudur stood before him, preparing a

117

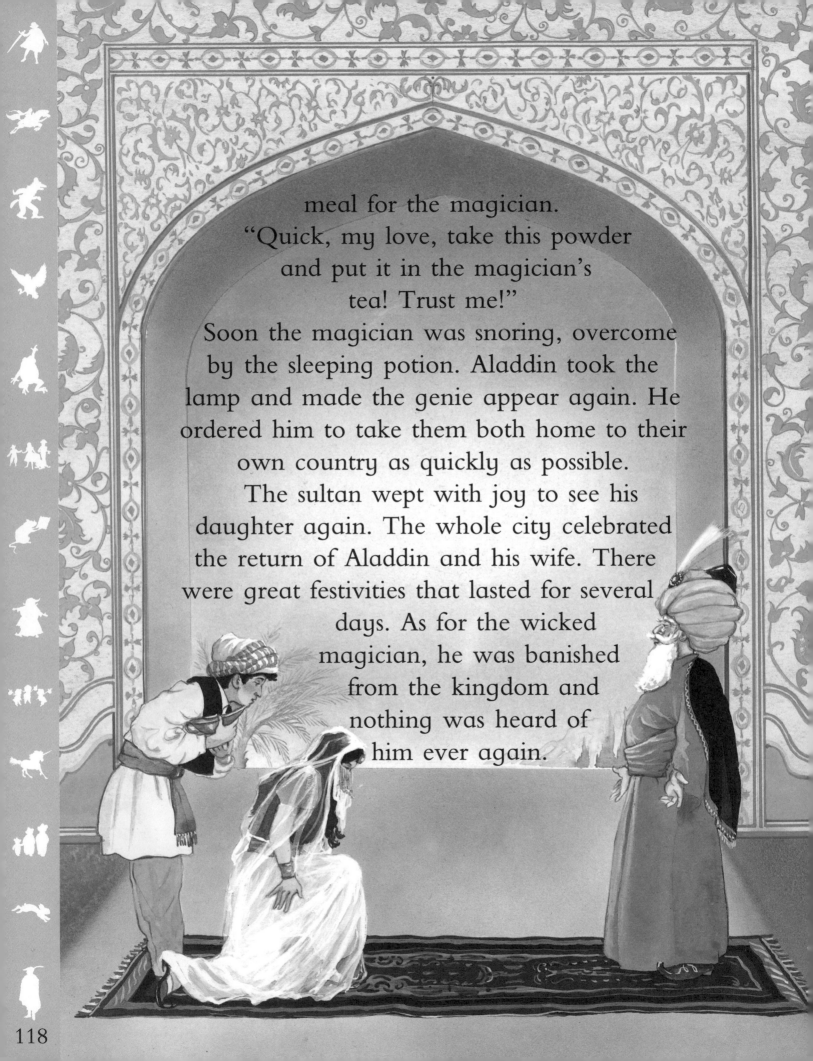

meal for the magician.
"Quick, my love, take this powder
and put it in the magician's
tea! Trust me!"
Soon the magician was snoring, overcome
by the sleeping potion. Aladdin took the
lamp and made the genie appear again. He
ordered him to take them both home to their
own country as quickly as possible.
The sultan wept with joy to see his
daughter again. The whole city celebrated
the return of Aladdin and his wife. There
were great festivities that lasted for several
days. As for the wicked
magician, he was banished
from the kingdom and
nothing was heard of
him ever again.

The Bluebird

Once upon a time there was a king. He had lost his wife, so he married again. His new wife was a poor widow. The king had a daughter named Florine, who was sweet and gentle. The new queen also had a daughter. She was nicknamed Troutlet, as she was rather ugly and very selfish.

The new queen and her daughter hated Florine. They were jealous of her beauty.

One day, a foreign prince named Prince Charming came to the royal castle. The queen decided that he should

119

marry her daughter,
Troutlet. But, when the young man saw Florine, he fell in
love with her at once. The queen was furious and locked
her stepdaughter up in a high tower. Then she decided to
trick Prince Charming. A lady-in-waiting told the prince
that on that very evening, Florine would be standing at a
window overlooking the garden, and that he would be able
to talk to her from there.

It was very dark that night, and Prince Charming did not
realize that he was declaring his love to Troutlet. He
promised to marry her and to take her far away from the
castle. Troutlet, her face hidden behind a black veil, took
the prince to her godmother, the wicked fairy Soussio.

"Prince Charming, this is Princess Troutlet. She is my

godchild and you have
promised to marry her,"
she told him.

The prince realised that he had been tricked and he tried
to run away, but the wicked fairy touched him and
immediately his feet were glued to the floor. The poor
prince cried out, "Even if you skin me alive, I shall never
belong to anyone but Florine." So the furious wicked fairy
changed the prince into a bluebird. The prince, finding that
he had been changed into a bird and that his body was
covered with blue feathers, gave a pitiful cry and
flew away.

Meanwhile, Florine wept bitterly in the tower, believing that the prince had married Troutlet. But one day, a bluebird

came and perched on a cypress tree outside her window. "I am your prince," he tweeted, and he told Florine how he had come to be a bird. From then on, every night Florine and the bluebird would meet, talk and try to console each other. The prince even brought her jewels all the way from his palace. But one evening, the wicked queen discovered what was happening. She ordered that sharp pieces of glass should be tied to the trees around the castle. Night fell and when the bluebird tried to perch in a tree, he cut his wings and feet. The prince thought that Florine had betrayed him in order to gain the wicked queen's favor. The dying prince managed to drag himself to his nest. By a stroke of luck, a magician was passing by and found him. He took the injured bluebird to his home and nursed him back to health. Florine, in despair at the disappearance of her prince, called out again and again, "Bluebird, bluebird, color of the sky, come to me as swiftly as you can fly!"

But her bluebird never returned.

Then Florine's father died and the people of his kingdom rose up and attacked the castle. The queen was taken prisoner, and Florine was rescued and crowned as the new queen. Florine was happy, but all she could think about was finding her Prince Charming. One night, she

took the emerald bracelets that the bluebird had given her and left on a secret mission to find him.

Meanwhile, the magician who was taking care of the injured bluebird went to look for the wicked fairy Soussio.

"The bluebird will never become Prince Charming again unless he marries Troutlet," she told him. So the magician persuaded the prince to marry the ugly Troutlet, to escape the wicked spell. Sadly he agreed to do this, and Prince Charming became a man once more.

That same day, the new Queen Florine, disguised as a peasant woman, reached the gates of Prince Charming's palace. There she learned that the prince was to marry Troutlet the very next day.

Florine was so sad. The man she loved had betrayed her. But remembering something the bluebird had told her, she decided to go and meet her rival.

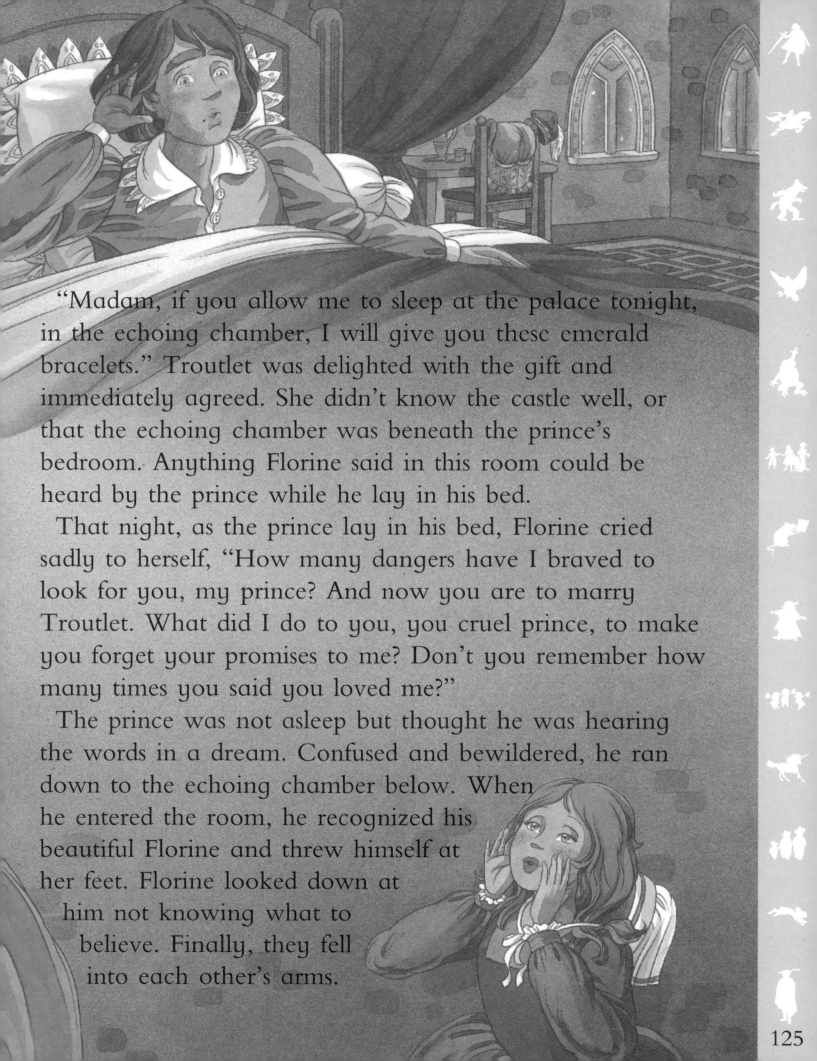

"Madam, if you allow me to sleep at the palace tonight, in the echoing chamber, I will give you these emerald bracelets." Troutlet was delighted with the gift and immediately agreed. She didn't know the castle well, or that the echoing chamber was beneath the prince's bedroom. Anything Florine said in this room could be heard by the prince while he lay in his bed.

That night, as the prince lay in his bed, Florine cried sadly to herself, "How many dangers have I braved to look for you, my prince? And now you are to marry Troutlet. What did I do to you, you cruel prince, to make you forget your promises to me? Don't you remember how many times you said you loved me?"

The prince was not asleep but thought he was hearing the words in a dream. Confused and bewildered, he ran down to the echoing chamber below. When he entered the room, he recognized his beautiful Florine and threw himself at her feet. Florine looked down at him not knowing what to believe. Finally, they fell into each other's arms.

At that moment, the magician arrived with a good fairy. They would use their magic powers to help Prince Charming and Queen Florine. As soon as it was morning, their wedding was announced to the whole palace. Troutlet was furious and ran to see the prince, but the magician and the good fairy quickly changed her into an ugly turkey.

The prince and his Queen Florine could think of nothing else but the preparations for their wedding and the happy years they could now spend together.

The Wild Swans

In a land far beyond the sea, there lived a king and queen who had eleven sons and one daughter called Elisa. The children lived happily until the day their mother died. Soon the king remarried, but his new wife was a wicked woman who immediately hated the twelve children.

In order to be rid of them, the evil queen decided to send the little girl to live with peasants, and said so many bad things to the king about his sons that he disinherited them.

But this was not enough for her. The queen wanted to send the sons away for good. So one day she cast a spell over them—because she was a witch—saying to them, "You will be changed into birds and lose the power of speech!" So the princes turned into eleven handsome wild swans who flew away at once.

When Elisa was fifteen years old, her father sent for her because he wanted to see his daughter again. But the evil queen waylaid her before she reached the castle. She stained the princess's face with walnut juice and tangled her hair so much that her father did not recognize her. The poor girl was very sad and left the castle to tramp home through the fields.

In the evening, Elisa came to a huge forest where she fell asleep. When she awoke, she found herself by a river of clear water. She leaped into the water and bathed. The dirt and stains were cleaned away and once again she became the beautiful princess she had been. The princess went on her way and met an old lady. Elisa asked her whether she had seen eleven princes riding through the forest. The old lady answered that she had not, but she had seen eleven wild swans wearing gold crowns standing on the seashore. The little girl followed the river until it flowed into the sea. On the beach, Elisa found eleven white swan feathers. At dusk, she saw eleven wild swans wearing gold crowns flying in formation like a long white ribbon. The swans flew down and perched next to her. As soon as the sun set, their feathers dropped from them and they became her eleven handsome brothers once more.

Elisa's eldest brother explained to her that they were able to regain human form as soon as night fell.

He added, "We live in a land across the sea and we can only come back to our beloved homeland for eight days each year."

Elisa's brothers wove a wicker hurdle on which to carry Elisa and, the next morning, they flew away with her, holding the hurdle in their beaks. They flew all day. Although Elisa's weight slowed their flight, they reached an island before nightfall. They were very tired and very soon they were all asleep.

While Elisa slept, a fairy named Morgan-le-Fée appeared in her dream and said, "You can save your brothers by making a coat of armour woven from nettles. But you must be careful; until the work is finished you must not speak, for if you do, it will cause their death."

Elisa went to work immediately, spinning and weaving the coats of armour until her hands were badly stung by the nettles. A king out hunting, saw the beautiful young girl hard at work and asked what she was doing. Elisa would not answer because she knew that if she uttered a single word, her brothers would die. Moved by the princess's obvious distress, the

king decided to take her away to his castle. Soon after, they married. But Elisa wept and lamented until the king had the idea of bringing her the nettles that she had already spun and the coats of armour she had already completed, hoping this would please her.

The king's court counselor was suspicious of the mute girl and wondered whether she might be a witch. He said so, but the king refused to listen.

Every night, Elisa worked on the coats of armour. One day, she ran out of nettles and decided to visit the cemetery to pick more. The counselor, who was spying on her, told the king, and when the young woman went out again to pick nettles, the king himself followed her. Seeing her standing near the cemetery, where witches

caught toads for their magic potions, the king agreed with his counselor. Elisa must be a witch.

Elisa was accused of witchcraft and was condemned to death. In her prison cell, she was given the coats of armour and the rest of the nettles, so she could continue her work, despite the fact that she might never see her brothers again.

On the day of her execution, Elisa was taken to the stake. Pale as death, the young queen, her hair tangled and unkempt, desperately continued to weave the last coat of armour.

"Look at the witch! Tear up her magic cloth!" shrieked the crowd. People ran up to her and tried to wrench the nettle cloth from her hands when, suddenly, eleven swans flew down and perched around her.

Elisa barely had the time to throw the eleven coats of armour

133

over the swans, but as she did so, they immediately changed back into handsome young men. The young queen exclaimed, "At last! I can speak and proclaim my innocence."

"Yes, our sister is innocent!" confirmed the oldest brother, who told the king the whole story. The king was delighted to be reunited with his young wife and presented her with a swan's feather that was floating in the air. The bells began to ring. The king and Elisa, accompanied by the eleven handsome princes, took the road back to the castle to hold a great celebration that lasted for eleven days and eleven nights.

Tom Thumb

A peasant couple lamented that they had no children. Then one day, the wife declared, "Even if I were to bear a child no bigger than a thumb, we would love it with all our hearts."

Her wish was granted and, because the boy was no bigger than a thumb, they named him Tom Thumb. Even as he grew older the little boy remained very tiny, but he was bright and alert.

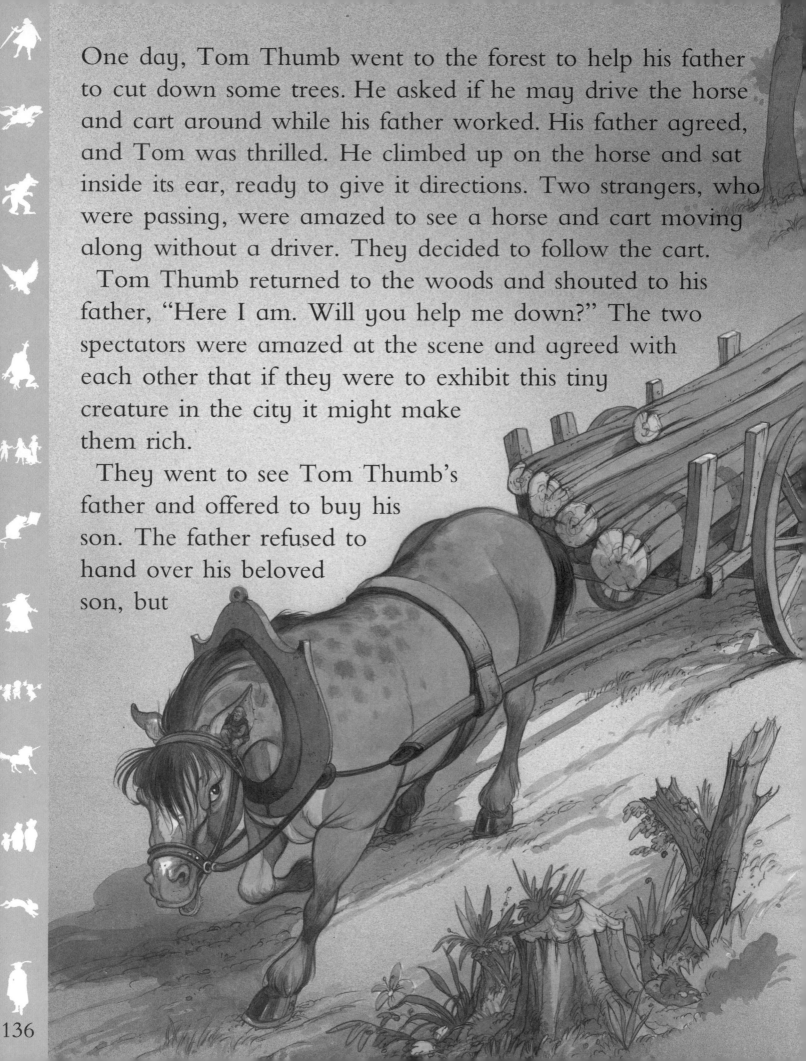

One day, Tom Thumb went to the forest to help his father to cut down some trees. He asked if he may drive the horse and cart around while his father worked. His father agreed, and Tom was thrilled. He climbed up on the horse and sat inside its ear, ready to give it directions. Two strangers, who were passing, were amazed to see a horse and cart moving along without a driver. They decided to follow the cart.

Tom Thumb returned to the woods and shouted to his father, "Here I am. Will you help me down?" The two spectators were amazed at the scene and agreed with each other that if they were to exhibit this tiny creature in the city it might make them rich.

They went to see Tom Thumb's father and offered to buy his son. The father refused to hand over his beloved son, but

Tom Thumb urged him
to accept. He told his father,
"Don't worry, I shall find my way home."
So Tom Thumb left with the men.

That evening, at the inn, he slipped down to the floor
and disappeared into a mouse hole where he could not be
seen by the two men. Night fell and Tom Thumb was just
wondering where he might find a place to sleep when he saw
an empty snail shell. He climbed inside and while he was
there he heard his two owners whispering together. They were
trying to work out how to steal money from the local priest.
Tom Thumb shouted to them from inside the snail shell,
"Take me with you and I'll help you."
The two men agreed. After
all, they had not
earned any
money

from the little boy so far. And so they made their way to the priest's house.

Tom Thumb slipped inside the house and shouted to them in a loud voice, "Do you want to take everything that is in here?" The two thieves were frightened and begged him to speak more quietly, but Tom Thumb began to shout again as loudly as he could.

The priest's housekeeper heard the voice and got out of bed to see what was happening. Hearing a noise, the two men ran off as fast as their legs would carry them, while the little boy hid in the barn. The housekeeper thought she must have been dreaming because she saw no one at all, and went back to bed after snuffing out her candle. Exhausted, Tom Thumb fell asleep in the hay and did not even wake up when the housekeeper came in to feed the cow in the early hours of the morning.

The woman happened to pick up the very bunch of hay on which the little boy was sleeping. He awoke horrified to find himself inside the mouth of the cow. But he was careful to avoid being ground by the animal's teeth and slid down into its stomach. It was very dark in there and he shouted out, "Don't send any more hay down here."

The housekeeper, who was tending the cow, recognized the voice she had heard the previous night and ran to tell the priest that the cow was speaking. At first the priest thought she was mad, but then he too heard Tom Thumb's voice. Believing the animal to be

139

bewitched, the priest ordered it to be killed, and thrown on a scrap heap.

A hungry wolf passing by swallowed the cow in a single mouthful. Brave as ever, Tom Thumb did not give up hope, but shouted to the wolf from deep in his stomach, "Dear wolf, I know where you can get a good meal." The wolf listened with interest to Tom Thumb as he described how to find his father's house, where the wolf would be able to eat all the stored provisions.

The next night, the wolf crept into Tom Thumb's home and ate so much that his belly dragged along the ground. He was so full that he could not move and so fat that he could not squeeze through the doorway.

Tom Thumb then began to jump about and shout loudly. "Be quiet, you'll wake everyone up," begged the frightened wolf.

But Tom Thumb replied that if the wolf had enjoyed himself so much, he also had the right to have fun, and he continued making a terrible din. The noise finally woke his parents and they came to the storeroom, where they looked in through a crack in the door.

Seeing the wolf, Tom Thumb's parents ran to fetch weapons. His father took an ax and his mother a scythe.

141

The father said to his wife, "I'll hit him first and if that doesn't kill him you can finish him off with the scythe." Hearing his father's voice, Tom Thumb cried out,

"Father, I am in the wolf's stomach!"

So he hit the wolf on the head and the animal fell down dead. Then his parents found the scissors and very carefully opened the animal's stomach. Tom Thumb threw himself into their arms and thankfully breathed in gulps of fresh air.

"But where did you go?" they asked him with great curiosity.

"I had lots of adventures, but I'm so happy that I'm home again!"

Tom Thumb's parents covered him with kisses. Then they washed him in a bowl of hot water and dressed him in brand new clothes.

The Tinderbox

There was once a brave soldier who was coming home from the wars. On the way, he met an ugly witch with a hooked nose and heavy lips. "Good day, soldier," she greeted him. "How handsome you are and how like a real fighting man. If you will do one thing for me, I shall give you as much money as you desire. But before I do so, you must do this thing for me. Climb to the top of that tree. There you will find a hole and you must squeeze into it. Inside, you must go down a corridor that is brilliantly lit by a hundred lamps. At the end of the corridor, you will find three doors behind which three treasures are hidden.

But beware! In front of each door there stands a fierce dog. Talk gently to each dog in turn and they will do you no harm. You can take all the silver you like, but in exchange, you must bring me back the tinderbox which my grandmother forgot on her last visit."

So that is what happened. The brave soldier climbed the tree, squeezed in through the hole, and found himself in a huge corridor at the end of which stood three big dogs.

"You are a fine fellow," said the young man to the first dog, and took the copper coins. "Take care you do not stare at me too hard, you might hurt your eyes," he said to the second dog, and he took the silver treasure. Then he smartly saluted the third dog and said to him, "Good evening," while taking the gold treasure which he guarded.

Before he returned, the soldier picked up the tinderbox that was lying on the floor.

The soldier's pockets were overflowing with copper, silver, and gold treasure. When he climbed out of the tree again, he asked the witch, "I have your tinderbox, but what will you do with it?"

The old woman refused to answer. Frustrated with her silence, the soldier pulled out his saber and killed her. He slung the treasure on his back, put the tinderbox in his pocket, and went to the town where he lived extravagantly for some time.

He visited the theater, hired a carriage to see the king's gardens, and often gave alms to the poor. Everyone loved the brave soldier, but he was very sad. He knew that the king's beautiful daughter was imprisoned in a copper castle somewhere in the kingdom.

No one was allowed to visit her. She had been imprisoned in the castle because it had been foreseen that one day she would marry a mere soldier. The king was so anxious that he had locked her up behind thick walls.

So the poor soldier was rich but unhappy! He carried on spending money thoughtlessly every day.

One day, he awoke to find all that remained of his fortune was two pennies. No more beautiful clothes and delicious food! So once more, the soldier lived in a tiny room under the eaves.

One dark evening, he did not even have enough money to buy a candle, but he suddenly remembered the tinderbox from the hollow tree.

So he struck the tinderbox and at once sparks flew from it.
Suddenly the door opened, and the first dog walked in saying,
"Master, what is your command?"

"Can I really have anything I want?" cried the soldier.
"Quickly, bring me some money." The second dog walked in
and he asked him, "Can you bring the beautiful princess
here?" Now the soldier realized the true value of the tinderbox.

If he struck it once, the dog who
guarded the copper coins would appear. If he struck it
twice, the dog who guarded the silver coins would also
appear. And if he struck it three times, the dog who
guarded the gold coins would appear too. The first dog
returned immediately, holding a huge sack full of gold,

silver, and precious stones in his mouth.

Then the young soldier quickly put on his handsome dress
uniform. He barely had time to finish dressing when the
second dog returned with the princess sitting on his back.
The soldier could not help kissing her, because she
was so beautiful.

That evening, the second dog took the beautiful princess
back to the copper castle. She returned the next day, then the
day after that, and so on, until the king, who was very

jealous, realized that something was afoot. He had his daughter followed by her ladies-in-waiting. The two lovers were discovered and the soldier was arrested, thrown into prison, and sentenced to death. Fortunately, the brave soldier had not forgotten his magic tinderbox.

Outside the town stood the gallows, surrounded by a huge crowd of people. The king and queen were seated on thrones.

The soldier was on the platform, and the rope was about to be placed around his neck when he asked to be allowed to smoke a last pipe. The king could not refuse, so the soldier took the tinder box and struck it—once, twice, three times!

And all at once, the three dogs appeared. "Come to my aid, they are going to hang me!" cried the young soldier. So the three big dogs fell upon the king and queen and tossed them high into the sky.

The people were so terrified they cried out, "Soldier, you shall be our king and you shall marry the beautiful princess."

The wedding festivities soon began and the dogs were honored guests. And the valiant soldier and his beautiful queen lived happily ever after.

The Little Match Girl

It was New Year's Eve, and the weather was bitterly cold. The sky was pitch black, and snow fell in large flakes. In the midst of the blizzard, a little girl staggered down the street, her head and feet bare. When she had left home, she had been wearing old slippers, but as she was crossing the road, she had been in such a hurry, that she had lost both of them. One of them had fallen right under the wheels of a large carriage, and the other had been grabbed by an urchin who wanted to use it as a boat.

The little girl
staggered along, her naked feet blue with cold.
In her torn and dirty apron, she carried a large bundle of
matches. She held a matchbox in her hand. She had had a
very bad day. No one had bought a single match from her.
She was cold and hungry and was frightened to go home,
because her father would beat her when he discovered she
had not earned a penny. The snow continued to fall and the
flakes looked like swan feathers in her pretty, curly, blonde
hair. But what did she care about having lovely hair? All
she knew was that on New Year's Eve all other little
children and their parents enjoyed a big celebration feast.

The little girl found a spot in between two houses where she sat down, becoming colder and more frozen. What was the point of going home where her father would be angry with her? In any case, it was almost as cold inside her home as outside, the wind whistled so sharply through the large cracks in the walls.

The little girl could hardly move, her fingers were so stiff with cold. She told herself that if she lit one match, just one, it would warm her up. So she struck a match. There was a joyful crackling and the flame rose, warm and bright in her hand. The little girl had a sudden vision that she was sitting in front of a large copper stove. She stretched out her feet to warm them.

Too late! The stove had disappeared. All that remained was the blackened stump of a match in her fingers.

The little girl decided to strike a second match. This time, the flame was even brighter and more beautiful. The little girl saw a room containing a table covered with beautiful china. A large roast goose, all brown and plump, lay on a handsome platter. Then, suddenly, the goose rolled off the table and disappeared. All that lay before the child was the

cold, gray street. It was unbearable. The little girl desperately wanted to find the copper stove that had crackled so joyfully and the tasty goose that had smelled so delicious... The little match seller struck a

third match and found herself transported immediately to a beautiful house that contained a shining Christmas tree, covered with glittering garlands and brightly colored balls. Fruit and toys hung from the branches. Children were dancing in a ring around the tree, and they took her hand and brought her into the circle. The little girl wanted to join in the dancing, but suddenly she was outside in the cold again.

The snow had stopped and the stars shone over the dark, deserted street. A few passersby, in a hurry to get back to their friends and family, rushed past without seeing the little girl, who huddled between two houses and stared at the sky.

A shooting star left a long and brilliant trail. The little girl knew that this meant someone was about to die. Her old grandmother, the only person who had ever been

kind to her,
had taught her this: if a star falls,
it means that a soul has gone to
God. She struck another match
and this time her grandmother
appeared to her, looking as
she used to, with her
sweet and gentle
expression.

"Grandmother,
take me away!"
begged the little
match girl. "Do not
leave me alone. I know that when
the match goes out, you will disappear
just like everything else I have seen until
now. Like the fire that burned so brightly, like
the goose that smelled so delicious, like the
Christmas tree, you will fly away and I shall be
left all alone in the dark street without anyone to
look after me."

Terrified at the idea of being abandoned once
again, the little girl lit not one solitary match, but
burned the whole box. Her grandmother
reappeared, looking so beautiful in her black velvet
gown, that she wore only on special occasions. The

old lady smiled tenderly at her granddaughter and took her in her arms. Then they flew away into the sky amid the brilliant glow of the matches, and were soon in heaven.

The dawn broke on New Year's Day. A passerby discovered the barefoot little girl with curly hair, lying dead in the snow. All around her lay spent matches.

The poor little girl wanted to warm herself, thought the man, little suspecting that the child had left this world in a blaze of light, safe in the arms of her grandmother.

Ali Baba and the Forty Thieves

Ali Baba and Cassim were two brothers who came from a humble home. Ali Baba lived with his wife in a little house. He earned his living by cutting wood in the forest and selling the logs in the marketplace.

Cassim had married the daughter of a rich merchant, who would inherit her father's wealth. He wore silken robes embroidered with silver and was proud of his luxurious home. He had never considered sharing his immense fortune with anyone, not even his less fortunate brother.

One day, late in the afternoon, Ali Baba, who had gathered a large amount of wood, was about to leave the forest when he saw horsemen galloping toward him.

"Are these bandits?" he asked himself. He climbed up a tree and hid there. Forty men with evil faces came closer. I must be right. They look just like thieves, said Ali Baba to himself. He was very impressed with the huge parcels and large chests with which the horses had also been loaded.

From his hideaway in the tree, Ali Baba could see and hear everything. The leader of the thieves walked over to a large door that was concealed in a nearby rock. He stood in front of it and bellowed, "Open Sesame!"

Hardly were these words spoken before the door slid open wide. The thirty-nine horsemen followed him inside the cave, where they hid the gold, silver, and other goods they had stolen, and the door closed behind them.

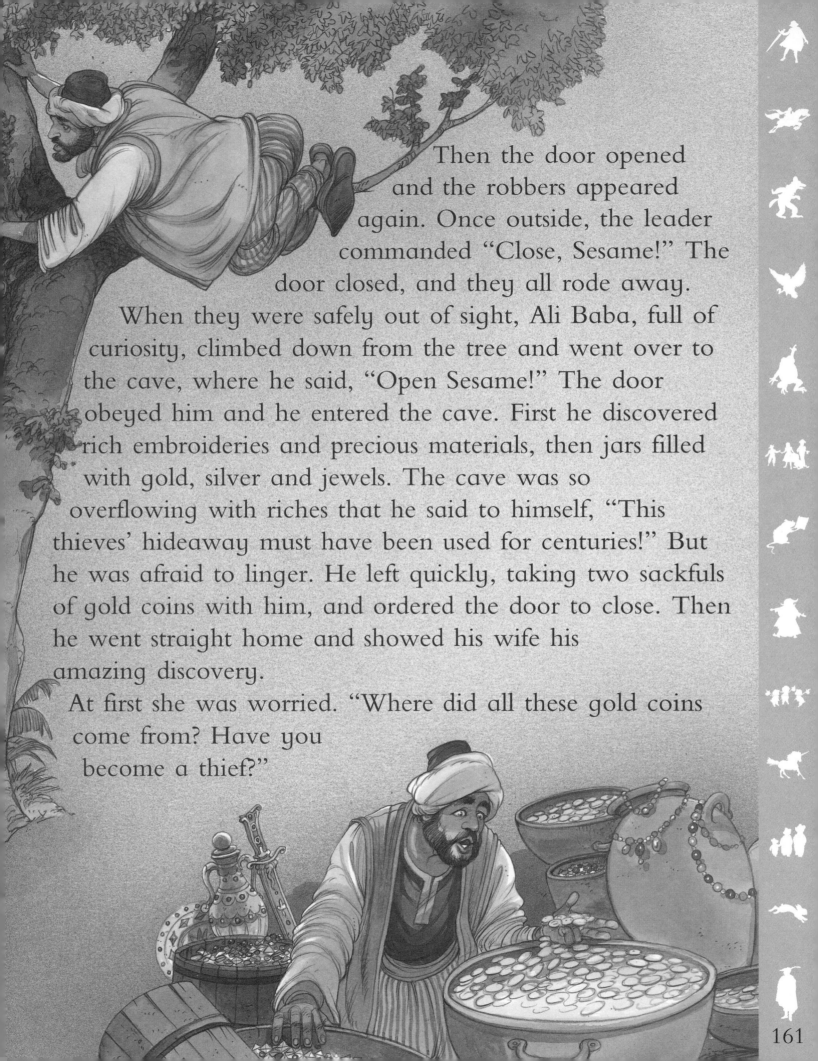

Then the door opened and the robbers appeared again. Once outside, the leader commanded "Close, Sesame!" The door closed, and they all rode away.

When they were safely out of sight, Ali Baba, full of curiosity, climbed down from the tree and went over to the cave, where he said, "Open Sesame!" The door obeyed him and he entered the cave. First he discovered rich embroideries and precious materials, then jars filled with gold, silver and jewels. The cave was so overflowing with riches that he said to himself, "This thieves' hideaway must have been used for centuries!" But he was afraid to linger. He left quickly, taking two sackfuls of gold coins with him, and ordered the door to close. Then he went straight home and showed his wife his amazing discovery.

At first she was worried. "Where did all these gold coins come from? Have you become a thief?"

161

"I have stolen them from thieves," he replied. He told her all about his adventure but asked her to keep it secret. Once he had reassured her, his wife began to wonder how much gold there was.

"We ought to weigh these coins," she said to him.

"No, no, we must bury them in the garden as quickly as possible," replied Ali Baba fearfully. But she begged and pleaded so much that he finally gave in.

"All right," he agreed. "I will wait until you have weighed the gold before I bury it."

This meant borrowing a pair of scales, so Ali Baba's wife went to see Cassim, her brother-in-law. Cassim's wife immediately agreed to lend her pair of scales. But her curiosity was aroused. She wondered what sort of grain the poor Ali Baba and his wife could be weighing. To satisfy her curiosity, she rubbed a little grease on the underside of the scales, so that a grain or two would stick to them. Then she gave the scales to Ali Baba's wife.

When the gold had been weighed, the scales were returned to Cassim's wife. But when she examined them, she saw that instead of grain, a gold coin had stuck to the underside of the scales!

She ran quickly to her husband. "Cassim," she cried, "you will never guess what sort of grain your brother has stored. A very strange sort indeed. It is gold! Your brother has so much gold that he doesn't even bother to count it, he prefers to weigh it!"

Cassim could not believe his ears. He hurried over to see Ali Baba. "My wife has found a gold coin on the scales she lent you. Where did you get gold from, you who never has two pennies to rub together?"

Ali Baba, realizing he had been found out, decided to confide in his brother and told him of the secret cave.

"Quick, tell me where it is," demanded Cassim.

So Ali Baba showed him the way.

The next day, Cassim rose before dawn. He made his way through the forest and arrived at the cave. He said the magic words his brother had told him to say and found his way in. At the sight of so much treasure, Cassim began to run around in all directions, to leap about and laugh out loud. He spent a long time exploring all the nooks and crannies in the cave.

Then he decided that the time had come to take away what he wanted and go home. He dragged out four sacks of gold coins and made for the door. As usual, the door had closed behind the visitor, and the magic words had to be repeated. "Open up!" ordered Cassim. But those were not the right words.

"Come on… open wheat!" The door remained shut. "Open barley!" Nothing happened.

He tried the names of various cereals. But while he was still trying to remember the right words, he heard the sound of horsemen approaching. It was the forty thieves who had come to store more of their loot.

"Open Sesame!" ordered their leader. The door opened, revealing a horrified Cassim. "How did this scoundrel manage to get in?" shouted the leader. "Get rid of him!"

The thieves hurled themselves upon Cassim and killed him on the spot.

They cut his body into four pieces, then placed the pieces on each side of the entrance to the cave, to warn others to keep away.

Once their bloodthirsty deed was done, they left.

When Cassim did not return, his wife went to tell Ali Baba that her husband was missing. So Ali Baba rushed to the thieves' cave and discovered his brother's remains.

As soon as she learned that he was dead, Cassim's wife wept bitterly. Ali Baba suggested that he take her as a second wife, as it was perfectly normal in that country to have two or more wives.

She agreed, and Ali Baba lived happily with his two wives. They kept their secret for ever, although from time to time they would visit the cave to get fresh supplies.

Little Red Riding Hood

Once upon a time there lived a little girl who was loved by everyone, especially by her grandmother. One day the old lady gave her granddaughter a red velvet cloak that suited her so well that the little girl did not want to take it off. So she became known as Little Red Riding Hood. One fine morning her mother said, "Little Red Riding Hood, here is a cake and a jug of elderberry wine to take to your grandmother who is ill in bed. Go quickly before the day gets too hot, and don't hop and skip on the way or you might break the jug."

Little Red Riding Hood promised to be careful, then saying good-bye to her mother she set off.

Her grandmother lived in the forest, and it was a long walk from the village. On the way, the little girl met a wolf. She didn't know what a wicked animal he was so she wasn't at all frightened.

"Good morning Little Red Riding Hood," said the wolf.

"Good morning," replied Little Red Riding Hood, politely.

"And where are you going so early in the morning?"

"To see my grandmother."

"And what are you carrying in your basket?" asked the wolf. "A jug of elderberry wine and some cake we baked yesterday. They're for my grandmother who is ill in bed," she replied. "And where does your grandmother live?"

"Her house is in the forest, just a little way from here, under three big oak trees. You can't miss it," said Little Red Riding Hood.

"What a choice morsel this plump little girl is!" thought the wolf.

She's bound to taste better than her grandmother. I must find a way to eat both of them.

They walked on together for a while in silence, then at last the wolf said softly,

"Little Red Riding Hood, the forest is so beautiful yet you walk straight ahead as if you are going to school. Look around at all these pretty flowers and listen to the birds singing in the trees."

Little Red Riding Hood looked up and saw the sun's rays shining through the trees and pretty wild flowers growing everywhere.

My grandmother would like a bunch of these, she thought. It's not late, I've plenty of time. So she left the path and skipped off into the undergrowth.

169

As soon as she had picked one flower, she saw another, even prettier farther on, and went to pick that too. Without realizing it, she was wandering deeper and deeper into the forest.

Meanwhile, the wolf ran straight to the old lady's house and knocked at the door.

"Who's there?" said Grandmother.

"It's me, Little Red Riding Hood," said the wolf. "I've brought you some cake and elderberry wine."

"I'm too weak to get up. Just lift the latch," Grandmother called out.

The wolf lifted the latch and went in. He ran straight over to the old lady's bed and ate her up.

Then he put on her nightdress and lace nightcap and got into her bed, drawing the curtains around it.

Meanwhile, Little Red Riding Hood had picked such a large bunch of flowers that she could hardly carry it and decided it was time to take it to her grandmother. She hurried back to the path, but when she arrived at the house she was surprised to find the door open. Everything seemed strange. She went over to the bed and said,

"Good morning, Grandmother!" There was no reply. She drew back the curtains and saw her grandmother lying there with her lace nightcap pulled right down to her eyes, hiding nearly all of her face.

"Oh! Grandmother, what big ears you have," she said.

"All the better to hear you with, my child!" replied the voice beneath the nightcap.

"Oh! Grandmother, what big eyes you have."

"All the better to see you with, my child!"

"Oh! Grandmother, what big hands you've got!"

"All the better to hug you with, my child."

"Oh! Grandmother, what a big mouth and what big teeth you have!"

"All the better to eat you with," cried the wolf and he leaped out of bed and swallowed Little Red Riding Hood whole.

Then feeling rather full, the wolf climbed back into bed
and started to snore.

A passing huntsman heard him and thought,

Why is the old lady snoring so loudly? I will go and see
if she needs anything.

He went into the bedroom and saw the wolf fast asleep
in the bed.

"Ah ha, you villain! Got you at last!" cried the
huntsman. And he pointed his gun at the wolf and then
suddenly thought,

What if the wolf has eaten the old lady?

He put down his gun, took out a pair of scissors and started cutting open the sleeping wolf's stomach.

At the third snip Little Red Riding Hood jumped out.

"Oh what a fright I've had! It was so dark inside the wicked wolf!" she cried. Then her grandmother appeared, still alive, but scarcely able to breathe. The huntsman had arrived just in time!

Everyone was very happy. The huntsman took the wolfskin and went home. Grandmother ate the cake and drank the elderberry wine that her granddaughter had brought her and felt much, much better. Little Red Riding Hood said nothing, but promised herself that she would never wander from the pathway to play in the forest, ever again.

Merlin the Magician

Once upon a time there was a young girl. She was an orphan and led a quiet life. One day she learned that she was to have a baby and when the child was born, a miracle occurred. From the very moment the child came into the world, he was able to speak in many different languages. This amazing

child was christened Merlin. Years passed, and as he grew his special gifts came to light. Merlin could read people's thoughts and change himself into different shapes. He had become a magician.

One day, Uther Pendragon, the king of Wales, died. The lords of the country asked Merlin to choose a new king for the throne.

"Let's wait until Christmas," answered the magician. On Christmas Eve, all the lords assembled. Among them was Arthur, who was soon to become a Knight of the Round Table. When they all left the church after prayers, the crowd was amazed to find a huge carved stone in the middle of the town square. It was so enormous that

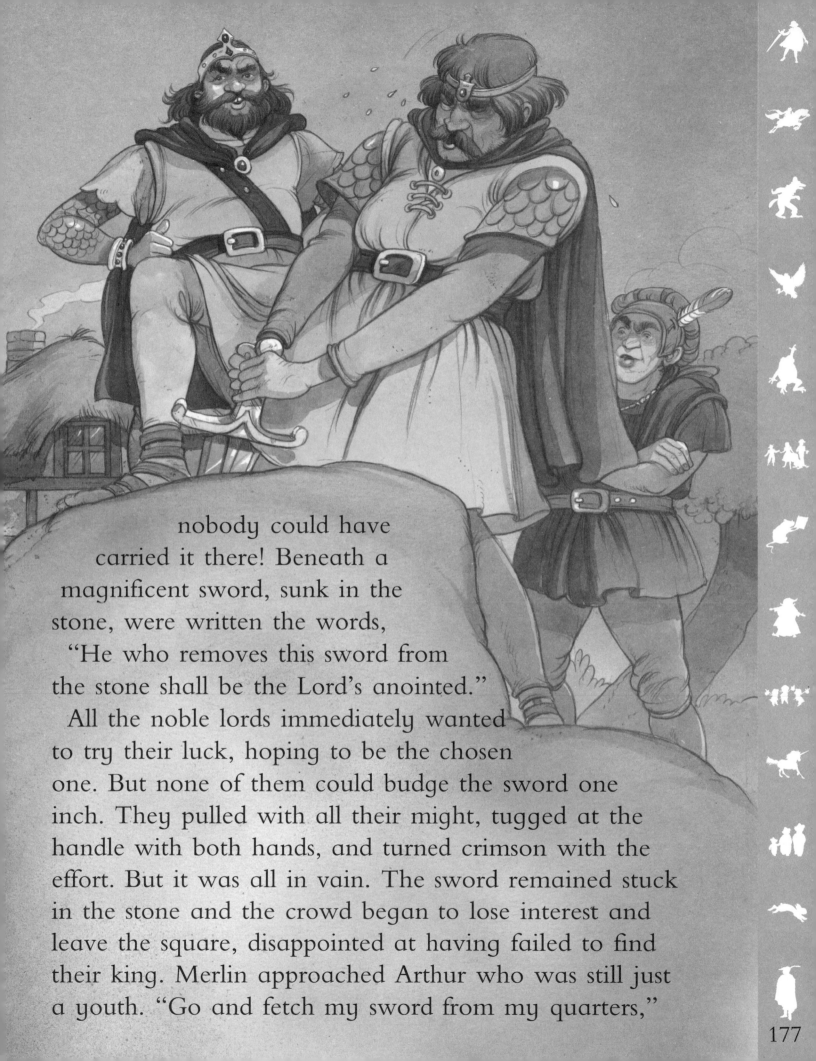

nobody could have
carried it there! Beneath a
magnificent sword, sunk in the
stone, were written the words,
"He who removes this sword from
the stone shall be the Lord's anointed."
All the noble lords immediately wanted
to try their luck, hoping to be the chosen
one. But none of them could budge the sword one
inch. They pulled with all their might, tugged at the
handle with both hands, and turned crimson with the
effort. But it was all in vain. The sword remained stuck
in the stone and the crowd began to lose interest and
leave the square, disappointed at having failed to find
their king. Merlin approached Arthur who was still just
a youth. "Go and fetch my sword from my quarters,"

Merlin asked Arthur.

"Gladly," answered the youth. Arthur saddled his horse and sped toward the magician's lodge. But he could not find the magician's sword at all. Frustrated he returned, passing the carved stone on his way. Taking his courage in his hands, he approached the stone, seized the huge sword in both hands and withdrew it without the slightest effort. Immediately, the stone vanished, as if by magic and the people, full of joy, greeted Arthur as their new king.

Some time after Arthur's coronation,

Merlin was riding through the woods of Avalon, admiring the scenery. He came to a fountain where a young girl was seated by the clear, pure water. She was so beautiful and sweet that Merlin decided to woo her by teaching her some spells. He taught her many things, such as how to transport a castle from one place to another, how to walk on water without sinking or even getting wet, or how to create a spring of fresh pure water in the hottest and most desertlike of places.

"I promise that I will love you if you teach me just one more spell," declared Vivian, the beautiful damsel.

Merlin took out his magic wand. With one hand he drew a circle, and a crowd of ladies, knights, and lords emerged from the trees,

as though the forest were inhabited. Then a marvelous castle appeared surrounded by a magnificent garden full of sweet-scented flowers. Everything was magical. Everyone held hands and danced with such grace, but the castle, which was invisible to all but Merlin and Vivian, disappeared into the clear waters of the lake as quickly as it had appeared. And then Vivian asked, in her most coaxing tone, "Dear friend, how could I hold a man, without using a prison cell, walls, or chains, in such a way that he remains forever my captive and so he can never leave without my consent?"

At these words, Merlin lowered his head and sighed, for he knew what her plans were.

"I know well whom you wish to lock up forever, in this way. It is myself and your plan is very cruel.

Alas! My love for you is so strong that I must comply with your wish." Then Merlin taught her all the spells that he knew.

Some years later, a peasant entered the forest of Avalon. All of a sudden he heard a distant voice calling him, and at the same time he saw a kind of mist before him, in the air.

"Alas! Brave man," said the voice. "Go and tell King Arthur that Merlin the magician is forever held prisoner in a prison of mist. Vivian, the beautiful lady of the lake, has placed me here. Tell him what has happened to me. One day, when I was asleep in the forest, Vivian came to me and drew a magic circle around the bush under which I was sleeping. When I awoke, I found myself on a magnificent bed, in the most beautiful room that ever there was, but it was impossible to leave. Never again shall King Arthur see me. I am a prisoner for all eternity. Go! And God preserve the king and the kingdom of Logres and all his lords as the best that ever there were."

These were the last words of Merlin the magician, who was never seen again.

The Shepherdess and the Sweep

In the living room there was a very old cupboard, its wood black with age. It was carved all over with roses and tulips and little deer with large antlers. In the center of the cupboard was carved a funny little man who grinned unpleasantly. He had goat's hooves, horns on his forehead, and a very long beard. The children of the house called him the Grand-General-Commander-in-Chief Goatfoot.

Commander-in-Chief Goatfoot always stared at a chest of drawers on which stood a beautiful porcelain shepherdess. She wore a little hat and golden shoes, her dress was adorned with a rose and she carried a crook. Near her there was a little sweep, as black as coal, also made of porcelain. They were placed so close together that they had secretly become betrothed.

Not far from them stood an old Chinaman with a nodding head, also made of porcelain. He pretended to be the shepherdess's grandfather, and had nodded in consent when the Grand-General-Commander-in-Chief Goatfoot had asked him for the little shepherdess's hand in marriage.

"In him you will have a husband," said the old Chinaman to the shepherdess, "who will make you Lady-Grand-General-Commander-in-Chief Goatfoot. Tonight, as soon as the old cupboard creaks, you will marry each other, upon my word!" So saying, he nodded his head and fell asleep.

But the little shepherdess looked at her
beloved sweep and began to cry.
"I beg you, help me escape! We
can no longer stay here."
"As that is your wish,"
answered the sweep, "let us
leave at once!"

So this is what they did.
Soon they had reached the
floor. But when they
looked back at the chest of
drawers, they saw that the
old Chinaman had woken up
and his whole body was rocking.

The terrified little shepherdess
whispered, "How are we going to run away from him?"
"The best route is up the chimney," said the sweep.
"Are you brave enough to climb into the stove with me
and leave by the pipe? Once in the chimney, we will

186

climb so high that he will not be able to catch us. At the very top there is a hole that opens out on to the wide world."

He led her to the door of the stove. "How dark it is!" she cried. But she bravely followed him. "At last, we are in the chimney," he announced. "Look up there at that magnificent shining star."

There was indeed a blazing star that seemed to be showing them the way. They both crawled up the chimney. It was as if the climb would never end. But the little sweep lifted the shepherdess, held her and showed her the best places to put her delicate porcelain feet.

In this way they arrived at the top of the chimney pot where they sat down to rest a little.

The star-studded sky spread out above them and over
the roofs of the town. They looked all around them, as
far as they could see. The little shepherdess had never
imagined herself in this situation. Her head rested
against the sweep's shoulder, she started to cry.
"This is more than I can bear! The world is too vast.
Oh! If only I could be standing on my chest of drawers
once again! I will not be happy until I have returned
there. I followed you into the world, now if you love
me, take me back down!" The sweep tried to reason
with her, but she sobbed so hard that he had to give in.
So they climbed back down the chimney, through the

pipe, and, at last, reached the stove. They waited behind its door to listen to what was happening in the living room. As they heard no sound, they peeped around the door. Alas! The old Chinaman lay in the middle of the floor. He had fallen from the chest of drawers in his attempt to catch up with them and was broken into three pieces. His legs had become detached from the body and his head had rolled into a corner. The Grand-General-Commander-in-Chief Goatfoot, on the other hand, was still in the same place, with a thoughtful look on his face.

"This is horrible!" said the little shepherdess. "The old grandfather is broken in pieces and it is all my fault!" "He can be mended," said the sweep. "When we have glued his legs on and placed a small hook in his neck, he

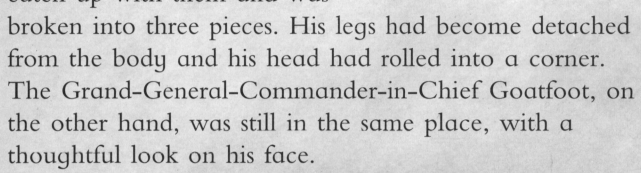

will be as good as new, so don't be sad. He will still be able to say lots of disagreeable things to us!" But when he was mended, the old Chinaman could no longer nod his head. "You have become very proud, since you broke into pieces!" said the Grand-General-Commander-in-Chief Goatfoot to him.

"Will I get the young lady—yes or no?"

The sweep and the little shepherdess threw the old Chinaman a pitiful look. They feared that he might nod. But he could not. His neck was held stiffly in place by a hook that had been used to mend him. Now nothing could keep the two porcelain figures apart. They loved each other tenderly . . . until the day when they too were broken.

Pinocchio

Once upon a time there was a lump of wood which fell into the hands of Gepetto, the carpenter. Gepetto's dream was to create a puppet that could dance and handle a sword. He would name this wooden puppet Pinocchio.

So, Gepetto started to carve his lump of wood. He carved hair, and then gave it a forehead and a mouth. Just as he had finished the face, he noticed that the puppet's eyes were moving. The puppet was alive, truly alive!

Delighted, the old man quickly carved the
neck, the shoulders, followed by the rest of the body. The
little puppet was hardly finished when he threw himself
into the carpenter's arms to kiss him and started to dance.
As Gepetto was very poor, he made Pinocchio some
clothes from paper, a pair of shoes from bark, and a hat
made from a loaf of bread.

To become a real little boy, Pinocchio had to go to
school. So the very next day, with a nice new notebook
under his arm, the puppet set off. On the way he met a
peasant who was so ugly that it was scary to look at him.
His long beard was blacker than an ink blot. His eyes
sparkled like red lanterns. Terrified, Pinocchio fled and ran
as far as his wooden legs would carry him. He
reached a field where he found five gold coins.

He decided to take these back to his poor father, the carpenter. But at the edge of the wood, Pinocchio met an injured fox and a blind cat who were limping along together.

"Hello, Pinocchio," said the fox. "My, what pretty gold coins you have. Would you like to make a thousand coins from your meager five? Well, at the foot of the Ninnies, there is a magic field that everyone calls the Field of Miracles. If you dig a hole and plant a single gold coin, you will find there, the following day, a tree laden with as many gold coins as there are grains on an ear of corn."

"Let's go there immediately!" exclaimed Pinocchio, forgetting all his good intentions about going to school.

And they walked and walked. At twilight, his friends abandoned him, saying they had to go and see someone. So Pinocchio continued along the path alone, in the dense, dark forest. Suddenly two menacing figures leaped out at him from the undergrowth.

"Your money or your life!" shouted the robbers, who were really the fox and the cat, disguised as robbers. The puppet ran away through the forest. But suddenly, a trap closed around his heel. Pinocchio was seized by such a fit of trembling that every joint in his wooden legs rattled. As if by magic, a child appeared. She was as beautiful as an angel, with blue hair and a face as white as wax.

She freed the puppet from the trap and told him in an
enchanting voice, "Little Pinocchio, take the gold coins to
your father."

"I have lost them," lied Pinocchio, who really had them
in his pocket. Hardly had he uttered these words than his
nose, which was already long, became even longer. It
became so long that he could not turn his head without
knocking his nose! The beautiful child, who was really a
fairy, began to laugh.

"Why are you laughing," asked Pinocchio, suddenly
embarrassed.

"I am laughing at the lies that you dare to tell me."
But taking pity on him, the little fairy clapped three times
and Pinocchio's enormous nose returned to its normal size.

"It serves me right!" the puppet wailed. "I wanted to be
lazy and to have fun, but I followed the advice of
dishonest friends. Bad luck has been following me
around. If I had stayed at my father's house, I would not
be so unhappy!"

And he promised the fairy that he would be a good boy and would work hard at school. Before vanishing, the fairy clapped one last time and a pigeon appeared in the sky.

"Pinocchio, come with me," it said, "I have just seen Gepetto. He is building a boat in which to travel across the ocean in search of you. He is prepared to face storms and gales just to find you again! We must save him before it is too late."

Pinocchio sat on the pigeon's back, and they flew eastward. Gepetto had already reached the open sea, and Pinocchio watched in horror as a wave larger than any of the others tipped the frail little boat on its side. The boat sank and Gepetto did not reappear.

"I fear that your father has been swallowed by the terrible shark," lamented the pigeon. "This monster is larger than a five-story house. His mouth is so large and so deep that a carriage with sixteen horses could fit inside." Frightened by these words, Pinocchio lost his balance and fell into the sea. Luckily, the wooden puppet knew how to swim, so he tried to reach an island on the horizon. But the terrible shark headed straight for him and swallowed him so roughly that he was knocked unconscious.

Pinocchio finally woke up and saw a faint glow, deep within the monster's stomach. And at the end of a tunnel he found his father, sitting there exhausted.

"Dear father! I have finally found you. From now on I will be a good boy! Now, let's make our escape while the shark is sleeping."

Together they climbed up into the monster's mouth. There, they crept across its tongue and climbed over the three rows of teeth. Pinocchio threw himself in the water, took his father on his back, and began to swim. Reaching the shore of the far-off island, they fell into a deep sleep. The puppet dreamed of the beautiful child with blue hair, and when he awoke, his eyes opened wide! He was no longer a puppet but a real little boy.

Thumbelina

Once upon a time there was a woman who longed for a tiny little child. But she was not sure whether she would be able to have one. So she went to see the old village witch and said to her, "I beg you to help me have a child!"

The witch gave her a grain of barley and told her to plant it. It was a magic grain. The woman placed it in a pot from which a beautiful flower soon grew, whose petals were tightly closed.

"What a pretty flower!" said the woman as she kissed it. Immediately, there was a small explosion, the flower opened, and a tiny girl appeared. She was no taller than a thumb. Her mother named her Thumbelina and put her to bed in a walnut shell, which served as her cradle.

One night, when Thumbelina was fast asleep, a wicked toad came through the window. She seized the nut shell and took it to the marsh where she lived.

"Look, my son, at the pretty bride I have found for you!"

But the toad's son, who was as ugly as his mother, could only say, "Croak, croak, brekke. . . kex," when he saw her.

"We will put her on a water lily pad. It will be an island from which she cannot escape," said his mother.

The following morning, when she saw where she

was, Thumbelina began to weep.

"Do not cry, little one! Look at my son instead.
He will be your husband and you will have a lovely
home in the riverbed's mud," said the mother toad.

"Croak, croak, brekke. . . kex," said the son approvingly.
The poor little girl sat on the water-lily and cried so hard
that even the fish were moved. "Such a pretty little girl
cannot marry that hideous toad," they said. So they
nibbled away, beneath the water, at the stem of the lily

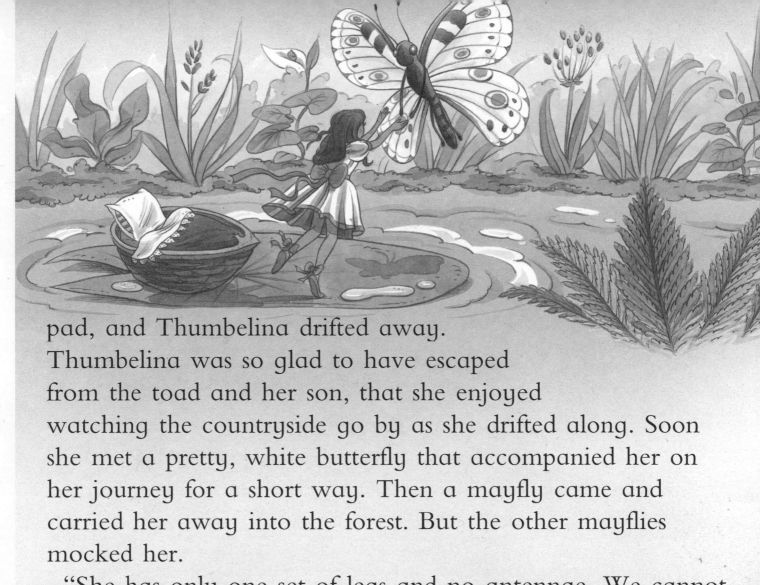

pad, and Thumbelina drifted away.
Thumbelina was so glad to have escaped
from the toad and her son, that she enjoyed
watching the countryside go by as she drifted along. Soon
she met a pretty, white butterfly that accompanied her on
her journey for a short way. Then a mayfly came and
carried her away into the forest. But the other mayflies
mocked her.

"She has only one set of legs and no antennae. We cannot

keep her with us."
So Thumbelina remained
alone in the forest. She drank the
morning dew and gathered the juice
from the wildflowers. She stayed
there all summer and fall. Then
came the freezing winter.
Thumbelina wrapped herself up in a
dead leaf and walked for a long time to find
shelter. At the edge of the woods, she came to the door of
a dormouse's home. It was a small hole hidden by some
wisps of straw. "It is so cold," she said, weeping, "please
open the door."

"Come in, little one, come into the warmth of my room.
You can stay here all winter if you will do a little
housework and tell me pretty stories."

Thumbelina accepted gratefully.

One day, the dormouse said to her, "We are going to enjoy the company of my neighbor, the mole. He would make a very good husband for you, as he is very rich and very wise. But he is blind. You will have to tell him your most beautiful stories to entertain him."

"Ladies, come and visit my abode," said the mole with pride. And he led them through a long, dark tunnel. On the ground there was a dying bird.

"Do not stop for such a trifle," he said, "it is only a swallow." But Thumbelina did not like the mole's cold heart.

The following night, Thumbelina was unable to sleep because all she could think of was the swallow. She went down into the tunnel and placed her head on the dead bird's chest. The creature's heart was softly beating. Every night, Thumbelina returned and secretly nursed the

swallow, which slowly regained its strength.

"Soon spring will be here and I shall be able to fly away," said the swallow. "Would you like to come with me?"

"It would make the dormouse too sad," said Thumbelina.

"Think about it," said the swallow and flew away.

Thumbelina returned to the dormouse's home. The creature was very excited about Thumbelina's marriage to the mole, and was planning the celebrations.

"Good bye, dear sun!" said Thumbelina lifting her eyes to the sky. "I will be kept beneath ground and I will never see you again!"

"Tweet-tweet," sung the swallow above her head. "Thumbelina, instead of staying underground with that heartless mole, come and join me on my adventures."

Feeling happy once again, Thumbelina jumped on to the swallow's back. They flew through the air, over mountains, valleys and seas, to arrive in a hot country.

In this wonderful place, grew the most beautiful white flowers in all the world. Right inside the petals of one of the flowers there was a tiny man who was so transparent that he looked as if he were made of glass. He wore a crown on his head and had crystal wings. He bowed low to Thumbelina.

"Will you be my wife, and become queen of the flowers?" he asked.

"Yes, charming prince," answered Thumbelina.

White wings were placed on Thumbelina's back and she was able to fly from one flower to the next.

"Tweet-tweet," the swallow twittered, then he flew away to tell Thumbelina's mother that her tiny daughter was safe, and happy at last.

The Brave
Little Tailor

One beautiful summer morning, a little tailor was sewing by his window when an elderly lady passed by. "Lovely cream! Buy my lovely cream!" she cried.

He signaled to her. "Over here! Give me two spoonfuls." The old cream seller had hoped to sell a lot of cream, so she went on her way rather disappointed.

The tailor cut himself a slice of bread, spread it with cream and left it on the table. "I will eat that when I've finished this doublet," he told himself. When he wanted to eat the bread, he noticed that a cloud of flies had already started to feast on it. He picked up a tea towel, swiped them with a great blow, and counted seven dead flies.

"Seven in one go! How strong I am!" he told himself. "The whole town ought to know of my strength, maybe even the whole world!" So he left his shop and set off.

Walking through the forest, the little tailor met a giant. The tailor had recorded his great feat on his belt, and the giant read it and thought the tailor had knocked down seven men in one go.

"You must be very strong," said the giant, "but I bet you can't do this." The giant picked up a stone and squeezed it so hard that drops of water came out of it.

"Easy!" said the little tailor. He took a piece of cheese, squeezed it in his hand, and juice ran from it.

"Well done!" said the astonished giant. "Now let's see if you can throw a stone as far as I can."

The little tailor laughed as he answered, "I can throw this stone so far that it will not even land. Watch." And he threw a little bird that happened to be in his pocket.

"Well done," said the giant.

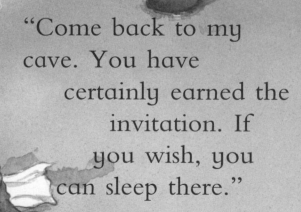

"Come back to my cave. You have certainly earned the invitation. If you wish, you can sleep there."

But, once night had fallen, the giant seized an iron bar and looked for the little tailor in the dark, in order to kill him. Seeing the giant, the little tailor ran off as fast as his legs would carry him.

He walked for a long time, finally falling asleep in a palace garden. Because of the inscription on his belt, he was mistaken for a great warrior, and he was asked if he would like to enter the king's army. "That is the reason I came," he answered. But the other servants, believing he could kill seven men in one go, were so scared of the little tailor that they abandoned their king. Regretting his decision, the king sought to get rid of the little tailor.

"As you are the strongest, go and kill the two giants who are terrifying my subjects. If you succeed, I will give you my daughter's hand in marriage and half my kingdom."

The little tailor found the giants asleep on the grass. He

climbed into a tree and threw stones at one of them.

"Hey!" the giant cried to the other. "Stop pestering me."

"I haven't done anything. Leave me to sleep in peace," answered the other giant.

"It can only be you. If you carry on, you will have me to deal with!"

They began to argue loudly and threw trees in each other's faces, killing each other. The little tailor, full of pride, returned to the king's palace. But the king went back on his promise and ordered the little tailor to kill the unicorn that was also plaguing his kingdom.

The unicorn, seeing the little tailor in the woods, started to charge him. As the animal was about to catch up with him, the tailor leaped behind a tree. Unable to stop, the unicorn thrust its horn into the trunk of the tree. Now the unicorn could no longer move, all the little tailor had to do was to kill it with his ax.

The king, unhappy at the thought of losing his daughter and his land, said to the tailor, "If you destroy the wild boar that is devastating my forests, I will keep my promise to you." The little tailor immediately returned to the woods to look for the wild boar. But the animal found him first, and the little tailor had to run as fast as his legs could carry him, with the wild boar at his heels.

Luckily, there was a chapel beside the path.

He ran into the chapel,
climbed out through a
small window and
rushed around to the
front to lock the door,
imprisoning the
boar inside.

The king could no
longer find a way to
avoid keeping his
promise, so he gave
his daughter to the
little tailor, with half
his kingdom. And that
is how the little tailor
became a king.

But the tailor talked
in his sleep, and one
night his wife heard
him muttering, "Patch
these breeches and sew up
this doublet for me quickly!"

She went to her father and
repeated these strange words.

"My daughter," said the king, "your husband is
nothing but a poor tailor! I have an idea. Tonight,
leave the door to your bedchamber open. Some men
will hide behind it, and they will deal with him."

But the new king's squire overheard the conversation

and he told the little tailor everything. The following night, the tailor pretended to fall asleep. Hearing a noise from behind the door, he said aloud, "I killed seven in one go and I have killed two giants, a unicorn, and a wild boar, so why should I be afraid of the men hiding behind the door?" On hearing these words, the men who were waiting to kill him ran away terrified. Since then, nobody ever dared challenge the cunning little tailor. He was able to lead a quiet life with his wife, who became very proud to have such a clever husband.

The Magic Horse

On the first day of every year, the king of Persia received all those who wished to see him. One year, an Indian man, holding a horse by its bridle, knelt before the king's throne.

"Your majesty," he said, "I should like to present you with a marvel that I created after many years of work. It is a mechanical horse that can fly. This horse can carry its rider to the other side of the world in an instant."

Prince Firouz, who was standing next to his father, exclaimed, "I want to try this horse!"

And without even stopping to put his feet in the stirrups, he leaped into the saddle.

"To start it, your highness, you need only press the button on the right, against the pommel of the saddle, then..."

The inventor did not have time to finish-the young prince had already pressed the button. In a single bound, the horse disappeared into the air.

"Wretch!" the king cried out. "You did not explain to my son how to return. If in three days the prince has not come back, I will have your head cut off. Guards, throw him in prison!"

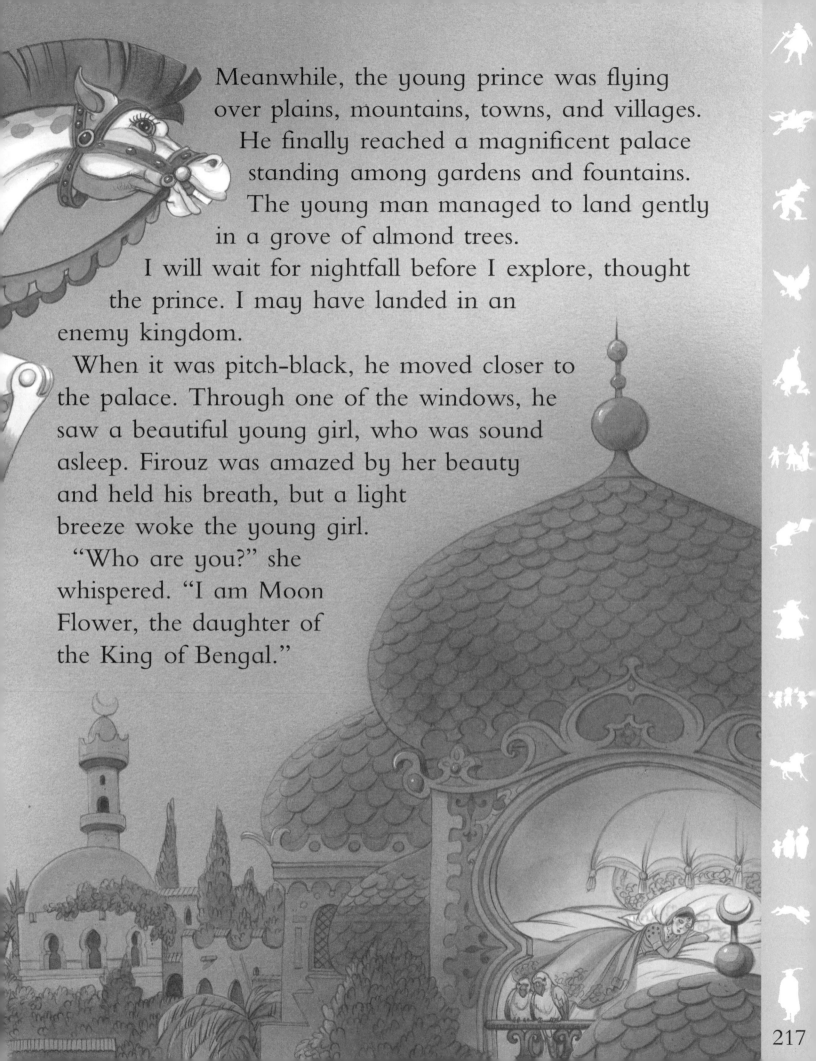

Meanwhile, the young prince was flying over plains, mountains, towns, and villages. He finally reached a magnificent palace standing among gardens and fountains. The young man managed to land gently in a grove of almond trees.

I will wait for nightfall before I explore, thought the prince. I may have landed in an enemy kingdom.

When it was pitch-black, he moved closer to the palace. Through one of the windows, he saw a beautiful young girl, who was sound asleep. Firouz was amazed by her beauty and held his breath, but a light breeze woke the young girl.

"Who are you?" she whispered. "I am Moon Flower, the daughter of the King of Bengal."

"And I am Firouz, the son of the King of Persia."

"You must have traveled a long way. If you like, you may stay in the palace for the night." The young girl rang a golden bell and some servants entered.

"Take the prince to the blue suite," she said. "You must be exhausted. Good night!"

Enchanted by the princess's beauty, Firouz was unable to sleep. The following morning, he told her his whole adventure and added, "I wish to return to my father's kingdom, but my strongest wish is that you come with me and become my wife." Moon Flower accepted, and without telling a soul, the two young people mounted the mechanical horse.

When the King of Persia saw his son returning with a beautiful princess, he was overcome with joy.

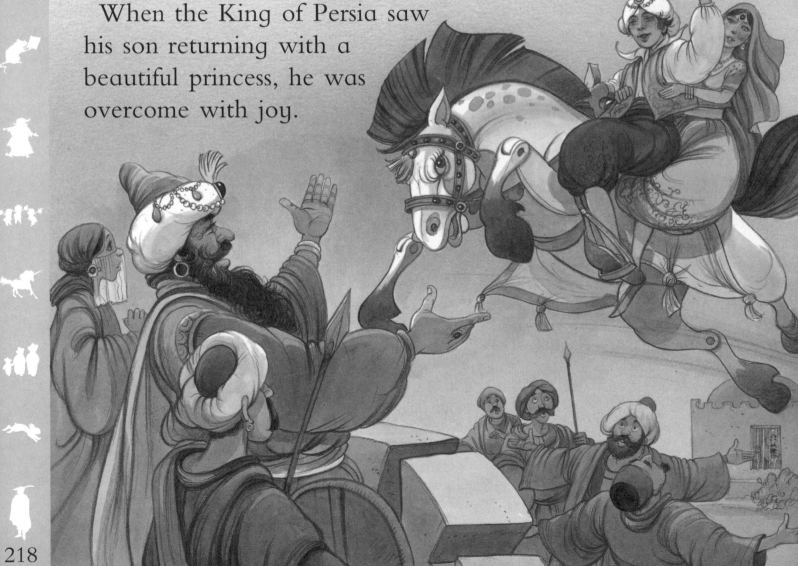

"Prepare a wedding banquet, release the
inventor from prison and may I never see him again."

But the inventor was so annoyed with this treatment, he
swore to take his revenge. He crept into the princess's
rooms and swept her up in his arms. He placed her on his
mechanical horse, and disappeared into the sky with her.
Discovering what had happened, the prince was determined
to find his princess again, and immediately set out.

Meanwhile, the inventor and the princess arrived in the
kingdom of Kashmir and landed in a vast forest.

"Wait for me here," said the man. "I will go and find
some food."

The princess started sobbing with despair. Her weeping
attracted the attention of the king of Kashmir who was
hunting in the forest. She threw herself at the king's feet.

"Save me!" she pleaded. "I have just been kidnapped by a
scoundrel." At that very moment, the inventor returned.
The hunters seized him and killed him at once.

The princess thanked the king and asked him to have the mechanical horse taken to his palace. The king, entranced by her beauty, swore to keep her for himself. He held sumptuous banquets and balls in her honor, but the princess became sadder and sadder. Her only thoughts were of her prince.

When he heard someone say the young prince's name, the king of Kashmir flew into a jealous rage. "I saved your life!" he shouted. "If you do not agree to marry me, you will remain locked up in this place forever."

In despair, the young girl pretended to have lost her reason. When the king came to visit her, she howled and stamped her foot.

Taken aback by this sudden change, the king called the

most learned doctors in the kingdom to come to examine
her. But none of them could cure the princess. Meanwhile,
Prince Firouz, who was traveling in disguise, had arrived
in the capital of Kashmir. Here the people talked of only
one thing – the madness of the unfortunate princess.
Firouz, realizing that they spoke of his lost love, thought, I
will rescue her and take her back to my father's kingdom,
where I will cure her with care and love.

He stuck a false beard on his chin, dressed himself in a
long robe, and went to the palace. Seeing yet another
doctor, the princess shrieked loudly.

"Leave us alone," said the disguised prince.

He tore off his false beard, and they fell into each other's
arms. "We must escape," said Firouz. "I have an idea."
Firouz went to find the king who was waiting for him.

"The young girl is the victim of an evil spell," said the
prince. "I will break the spell by burning the mechanical

horse, and the princess will be cured."

The following day, a huge fire was built in the main square. Firouz placed the princess on the horse and lit the fire. Then he uttered some magic words and threw some black powder into the flames. A huge cloud of smoke spread through the sky, and the king looked up in astonishment to see the mechanical horse rising above the smoke, taking Firouz and Moon Flower to freedom and happiness.

The Little Lead Soldier

Once upon a time there were twenty-five lead soldiers. They were brothers as they had all been made from the same old lead spoon. They stood with their guns shouldered, their heads proud, and their uniforms painted red and blue. The first thing they heard when the lid of their box was removed was a little boy, who had just received them for his birthday, shouting with joy. "Lead soldiers!"

The boy lined them up on the table. All the soldiers were identical, except for one, who had only one leg. Yet he stood as squarely on one leg as the others did on two.

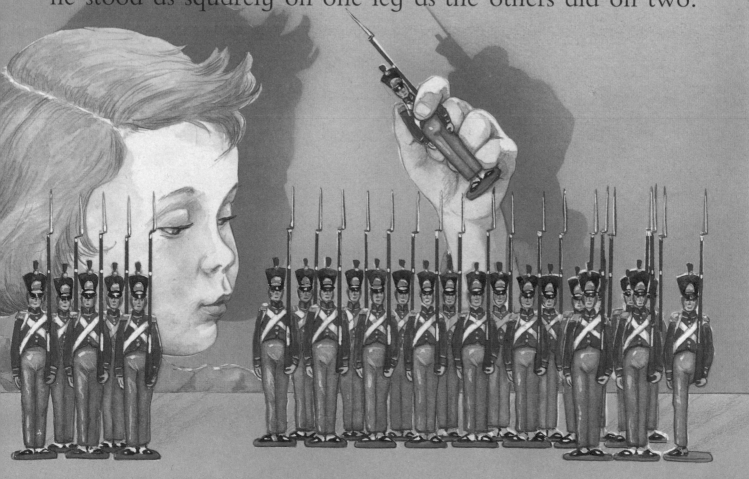

On the table where the soldiers stood, there were many other toys. The most remarkable was a cardboard castle. Through the little windows, one could see right into the rooms. Outside, small trees surrounded a mirror, which was the castle moat, on which wax swans glided.

The castle was very pretty, but what was even more delightful was the little dancer who stood by the castle gate. She, too, was made of cardboard. She wore a tutu, and for a scarf she had a thin blue ribbon decorated with a glittering sequin, as large as her face. The maiden stretched her arms above her head, because she was a ballerina, and she held one of her legs so high that the one-legged little lead soldier could not see it. He supposed that the maiden had only one leg like himself.

"She would make the ideal wife for me," he thought. Then he sighed. "But how elegant she is! She lives in a castle, and I only live in a box with twenty-four other soldiers. Nonetheless, I must try to make her acquaintance."

That evening, the other lead soldiers returned to their box, and the people who lived in the house went to sleep. Our little soldier hid behind a patterned wooden box.

On the stroke of midnight, there was a click!
  The lid flipped open and a little jack popped out. It was a jack-in-the-box.
  "Lead soldier," said the jack, "stop gazing at the little dancer and mind your own business!" But the little soldier pretended not to hear. "Wait and see what happens tomorrow!" continued the jack.

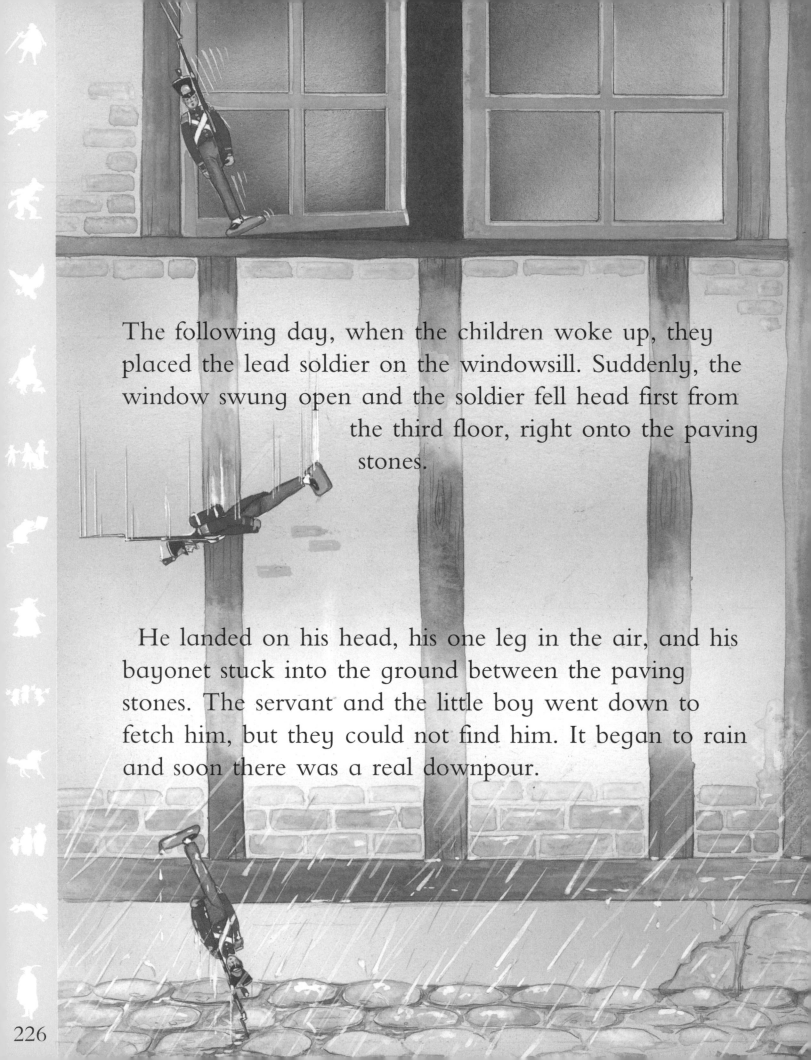

The following day, when the children woke up, they placed the lead soldier on the windowsill. Suddenly, the window swung open and the soldier fell head first from the third floor, right onto the paving stones.

He landed on his head, his one leg in the air, and his bayonet stuck into the ground between the paving stones. The servant and the little boy went down to fetch him, but they could not find him. It began to rain and soon there was a real downpour.

After the storm, two boys from the street passed by.
"Look," said one, "there's a lead soldier who is
begging to go for a sail." They made a boat from an
old newspaper, put the lead soldier in it, and launched it
in the water-filled gutter. The two boys followed him,
clapping their hands with glee. The lead soldier was
tossed about in all directions, but remained unhurt.
Suddenly, the boat slipped under a plank that was
covering the gutter and disappeared down the drain.
It is as dark in here as in my box, thought the lead
soldier. Where am I off to now? If only the little
dancer were here with me!

At the same moment a large rat appeared and shouted,
  "Passport! Passport! At the double!" The lead soldier did
not answer, but gripped his rifle tighter. The current was
already taking him toward the exit of the gutter that
flowed into the river. The boat wheeled around a few
times, took on water, and sank.

  Fortunately, the newspaper tore and the soldier managed
to escape. And at the very same moment, he was
swallowed by a large fish. It is even darker than before,
thought the lead soldier.

  But he stayed quite still, his weapon shouldered
as before. The fish was swimming about
violently in all directions.

Suddenly, it stopped leaping about. The lead soldier saw the light of day and heard a voice shouting,

"Look what I have found in this fish's stomach! A lead soldier!" It was the cook who had bought the fish from the market that morning.

She took the little soldier into the living room. At once, he recognized the children, their toys, the paper castle, and the charming little dancer. She had bravely stayed in the same position, her leg held in the air, which moved him very much. They gazed at each other but did not exchange a word.

Then, suddenly, and for no reason at all, the little boy seized the little soldier and threw him in the fire.

The little lead soldier was overcome by a terrible heat. He could feel himself melting. Little by little he lost his shape, but he continued to gaze at the little dancer. And, at that moment, the ballerina was caught in a draft and flew into the fire, next to the soldier. In a trice, she too had disappeared into the flames. The next morning, when the servant swept the ashes from the grate, she found a little lead heart and a sequin, which the fire had turned as black as coal.

Beauty and the Beast

Once upon a time there was a merchant who had three daughters. The two eldest daughters were very haughty, and were only concerned with their dresses and their jewelry. They never ceased to insult their little sister, who was gentle and kind. As she was also very beautiful, the youngest sister was named Beauty. She prepared the meals and did the housework while her sisters enjoyed themselves.

One day the merchant received a
letter informing him that he had to go
to town on business. The eldest
daughters were full of expectations and
asked their father to bring them new
clothes when he returned.

"I promise I will," he told them. "And
you, Beauty, don't you want anything?"

"Thank you, father," she answered, "but I need
nothing. However, should you find a rose, I would be
delighted to smell its delicate perfume." Their father left
for the town, but business being bad, he decided to
return home early.

On the way home through the forest, he suddenly saw
a bright light shining. Moving closer, he discovered a

magnificent palace. As its door was open, he entered and called out,

"Is anyone there?" But the palace was empty. He walked into the grounds and saw beautiful rosebushes growing beside the garden paths. Then he remembered Beauty's request and picked a rose for her.

At that very moment he heard a deafening noise. A huge beast appeared and cried out, "You have stolen a rose of mine, one of my most precious belongings!

For that, you must perish." He paused. "Unless you have a daughter who would be willing to die for you. If you have, go and fetch her and your life will be spared."

When he arrived home, the merchant told his daughters of the terrible thing that had happened. Beauty said to him, "Father, let me go in your place." The father cried out in protest, but Beauty would not listen to him.

The following day, she mounted her horse, and rode straight to the Beast's palace.

Once again, the palace seemed deserted. She entered and looked around. Inside there was a library and some magnificent furniture. At midday, she found a sumptuous meal laid out on the table and beautiful music delighted her throughout the meal. As dusk approached, she wondered when the Beast would finally appear. It was at nine o'clock when a tremendous noise made her tremble. The Beast was coming!

"Would it bother you if I watched you eat your evening meal?" asked the Beast.

"Master," answered Beauty, "you may do as you please."
"I am at your service," said the Beast, who added, "tell me truthfully, do you find me ugly?"

"You are ugly, but you are good-natured. You have treated me like a real princess." And she found that she was no longer afraid of him.

"Will you marry me?" the Beast asked her.

"No," she answered at once, surprised by the question. At that the Beast left, greatly saddened by her reply. Days passed. The most exquisite dishes were prepared for Beauty, and every morning she found magnificent new dresses, embroidered with gold. Each evening, the Beast asked her gently,

"Will you marry me?" And every time he received the same answer, which filled him with sorrow.
One evening the Beast asked her, "What else can I do to make you happy?"

"All I wish is to see my poor father again," she replied.

"In that case, promise me that you will return in eight days' time. Take this ring. As soon as you place it beside

your bed, you will be transported back here."

"I promise," said Beauty.

Then the Beast clicked his fingers, and Beauty suddenly found herself back at home. Her father held her in his arms for a long time. But her sisters were very displeased to see her. "Since she must go back in eight days' time, let's make sure that she stays here longer," they said to each other. "Then the Beast will seek revenge, and surely he will kill her."

On the eighth day, they pretended to mourn her departure. Beauty had begun to miss the Beast but felt sorry for her sisters and said, "I will stay just a little longer."

But then Beauty dreamed that the Beast had died of sorrow. Very worried, she laid the ring beside her bed and instantly found herself back in the palace. She searched for the Beast for a long time before finally finding him in the garden. Lying beside a stream, he looked as though he were dead. She splashed some water on his face, and the Beast opened his eyes.

"I thought you had forgotten me, and I felt I would die," said the Beast.

"Do not die. I want to marry you!" cried Beauty.

At these words, Beauty was astonished to find that instead of the Beast a handsome prince was gazing lovingly at her.

"What has happened to the Beast?" she asked him.

"He stands before you," the prince answered gently. "An evil fairy cast a spell on me and you have broken the curse, now that you have agreed to marry me."

And so Beauty and the Beast were married in a marvelous ceremony and lived a long and happy life together.

The Pied Piper

Once upon a time there was a town in Saxony called Hamelin. It was a small town, surrounded by high walls, and the people who lived there were very happy. But they were very greedy and loved to eat. It was said that the smell of their stews could be smelled over twenty miles away.

One cold Christmas Eve, as the moon shone brightly, the night watchman was doing his rounds, when he suddenly came to a halt. He rubbed his eyes, and opened and closed them a few times to make sure they were not deceiving him. He was not dreaming. A long black snake was coming across the frosty plain toward the town. And it was so long that its tail could not be seen.

But it was not a snake. It was a column of rats. The night watchman ran to ring the alarm bell at once. The rats were large, black, and hairy, with red eyes that shone like embers, and sharp, terrifying teeth! And there were thousands upon thousands of them, attracted by the appetizing smells of the Christmas feasts, biting, squealing and clambering over each other to reach the town. The dreadful sight made the hair of even the bravest men stand on end.

In a very short time, the rats reached the town, swam the moat, climbed the walls, and invaded all the houses. The awful black beasts ran into the kitchens, invaded the larders, threw themselves on the dishes that had been left on the tables and devoured everything they found.

There were hundreds, thousands, even millions of rats. It was a plague of rats. They ate everything. They ate all the food stored away for the winter. There was not a vault, cellar, nor sideboard, however securely locked, that was not visited. Nothing was left. Not even a crumb. So the burgomaster promised a reward of fifty florins to the person who could rid Hamelin of this plague.

It was on the morning of the third day that he entered the town. It is said that he was a tall, slim man with long, straight, jet-black hair and a green hat. He wore a satchel at his side. As soon as he arrived he asked to speak to the burgomaster.

"I have been told that there are fifty gold florins for whosoever rids you of the rats," said the newcomer.

"Prepare to pay!"

"What do you mean?" said the burgomaster. But the man was not listening. The townspeople watched him make for the town square and, there, take from his satchel a tiny black wooden flute, which he lifted to his lips and began to play.

Many years later, the people of Hamelin would tremble at the thought of that music. The mysterious player's slender fingers moved up and down the flute like a spider's legs and created eerie, haunting sounds that were so discordant they made people grate their teeth, and so sad that people's hearts throbbed.

Hardly had he begun to play than the sound of nibbling stopped. The rats appeared from everywhere and then, as the rhythm quickened, a sea of beasts, hideous and black, swarmed toward the piper.

They rushed, tumbling over each other, filling the streets to surround the flute-player. Then he started walking slowly toward the river, with the army of rats at his heels. The strains of the flute became aching and strange.

And all of a sudden, as though they had gone insane, the rats started to climb up the bridge's handrails, flinging themselves over in a turmoil of piercing shrieks, crashing on to the ice, which soon gave way beneath their weight.

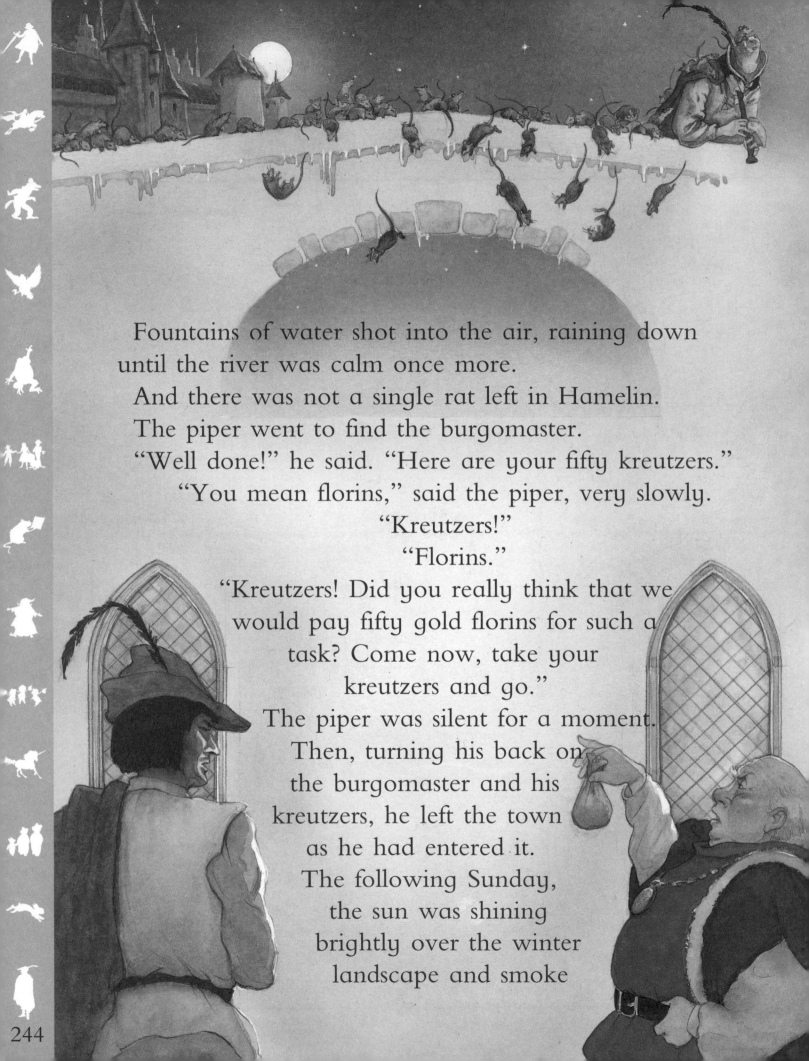

Fountains of water shot into the air, raining down
until the river was calm once more.

And there was not a single rat left in Hamelin.

The piper went to find the burgomaster.

"Well done!" he said. "Here are your fifty kreutzers."

"You mean florins," said the piper, very slowly.

"Kreutzers!"

"Florins."

"Kreutzers! Did you really think that we
would pay fifty gold florins for such a
task? Come now, take your
kreutzers and go."

The piper was silent for a moment.
Then, turning his back on
the burgomaster and his
kreutzers, he left the town
as he had entered it.

The following Sunday,
the sun was shining
brightly over the winter
landscape and smoke

could be seen rising from every chimney. In Hamelin's town square, the burgomaster was recounting, amid general laughter, the excellent trick he had played on the wretched piper and how, through his cunning, he had saved the town's coffers fifty gold florins. Then, all of a sudden, they saw him freeze, with his eyes open wide and his mouth gaping. Everybody turned around. The piper had returned. Without further warning, he put the flute to his lips. But this time he played an incredibly sweet tune.

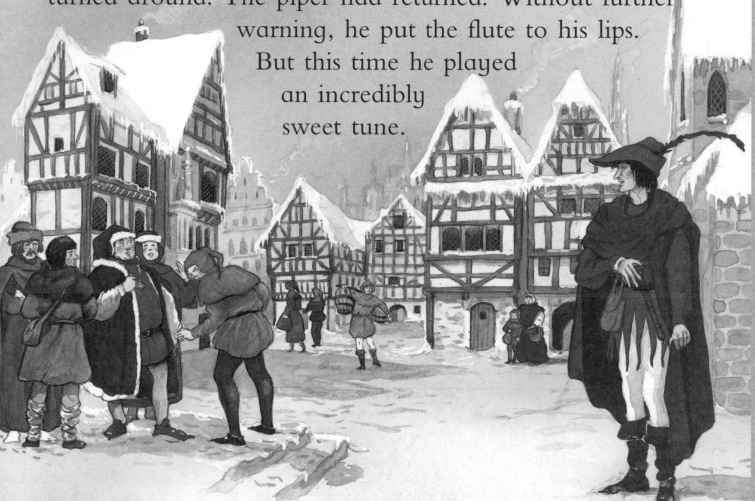

On hearing it, the townspeople immediately jumped up to dance and leap about. And the player's fingers leaped and danced along the keys of the flute, ever more agile and demented. And then all the children of Hamelin, even babies who hardly knew how to walk, flocked to the square from every part of the city, and

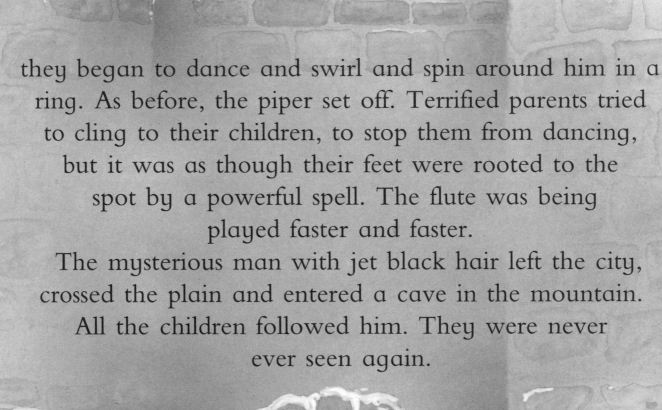

they began to dance and swirl and spin around him in a
ring. As before, the piper set off. Terrified parents tried
to cling to their children, to stop them from dancing,
but it was as though their feet were rooted to the
spot by a powerful spell. The flute was being
played faster and faster.
The mysterious man with jet black hair left the city,
crossed the plain and entered a cave in the mountain.
All the children followed him. They were never
ever seen again.

Jack and the Beanstalk

Jack lived with his mother in a little house. His mother did sewing to earn a living, while Jack tended the vegetable garden and looked after their only cow, Gentle, who he milked every day. That year, the winter was bitterly cold, and in spring hardly anything grew in the garden. One morning, Jack's mother told him with deep sadness, "We can no longer feed Gentle. We must go and sell her at the market."

And she asked Jack to take the poor animal to market.

"Try and get a good price for her," she advised him.

Jack left, leading Gentle on the end of a rope.

On his way to market, he met an old man dressed in rags.
"Where are you going with your pretty cow?"
he asked Jack.

"I am going to sell her at market," Jack answered,
"because my mother and I are in great need of money."

"I will buy her from you in exchange for these magic
beans," said the old man. "With their help, you and your
mother can forget all your worries." Jack was very eager
to please his mother, so he agreed on the spot.

"But watch out!" added the old man. "Using these
beans, you will be able to find some treasure that was
stolen from me a long time ago by a terrible and greedy
giant. If you can find it, the treasure is yours."

"Wonderful!" replied Jack, happy to have sold the cow,
he was in a hurry to get home with the good news.

When his mother discovered that Jack had come home
with just a handful of beans and no money, she was
furious and shouted, "Go straight to bed! There's nothing

for dinner." And in despair, she flung the beans out of the
window. The following morning, Jack woke up early. He
was quite surprised to find that there was something
outside his window which was blocking the light.
Opening his eyes wide, he realised with amazement that
a giant plant with huge leaves had grown up during the
night. It was an enormous beanstalk!

Jack opened the window and looked up,
but he could not even see the top of
the beanstalk.

249

Jack stepped onto the first leaf and began to climb upwards.

"The treasure must be up there," he thought.

He climbed through the clouds which, as if by magic, turned into beautiful countryside. He jumped down from the beanstalk and wandered off across the fields. He hoped to find something to quench his thirst and for something to eat, because he hadn't eaten since the previous day. He walked for more than two hours when, exhausted, he came upon a huge house.

He knocked on the door and a servant opened it.

"I'm thirsty and hungry, and I'm tired," he told the young woman, "may I come in to rest?"

"I would willingly offer you a place to rest, little boy, but my master is a giant who has eaten several children already. If you come in here, it will be the end of you!"

Jack felt like crying. But, from the floor above, he heard a thundering voice,

"Well? When is my dinner going to be ready?"

"In a minute, Sir!" answered the servant. She caught Jack by the hand and opened the door to the larder.

"Hide right at the back!" she whispered.

The giant was coming thundering down the stairs.

"Fee, fi, fo, fum! I smell the blood of an Englishman! You have let someone in!"

"Indeed not, Sir," said the servant. "It must be the smell of the meat that I have cooked for you."

"I doubt that!" said the giant. And he

started to search every corner of the room,
shouting all the time, "Fee, fi, fo, fum! I smell the
blood of an Englishman!" He opened the cupboards
and looked under the kitchen dresser. Jack stayed hidden
behind a stack of hams and trembled like a leaf.

"Come now, sir," said the servant, "your food will
get cold."

"Well hurry up and serve me then!" he boomed.

She filled his gigantic plate and placed on the table
three legs of mutton, a haunch of venison, four turkeys
and two dozen slices of roast beef. After this huge meal,
the giant called to his servant, "Bring me my gold coins,

Index of Stories

so long to pick himself up that Jack had a good lead.
Jack easily beat the giant to the beanstalk, jumped on to
it and slid down, all in one go. But the giant was so heavy
that, as he grabbed hold of the beanstalk, the stem bent
towards the sea, and he lost his balance and fell into the
ocean and drowned. When Jack arrived home, his mother
welcomed him with cries of joy. With the gold they could
buy everything that they ever wanted!

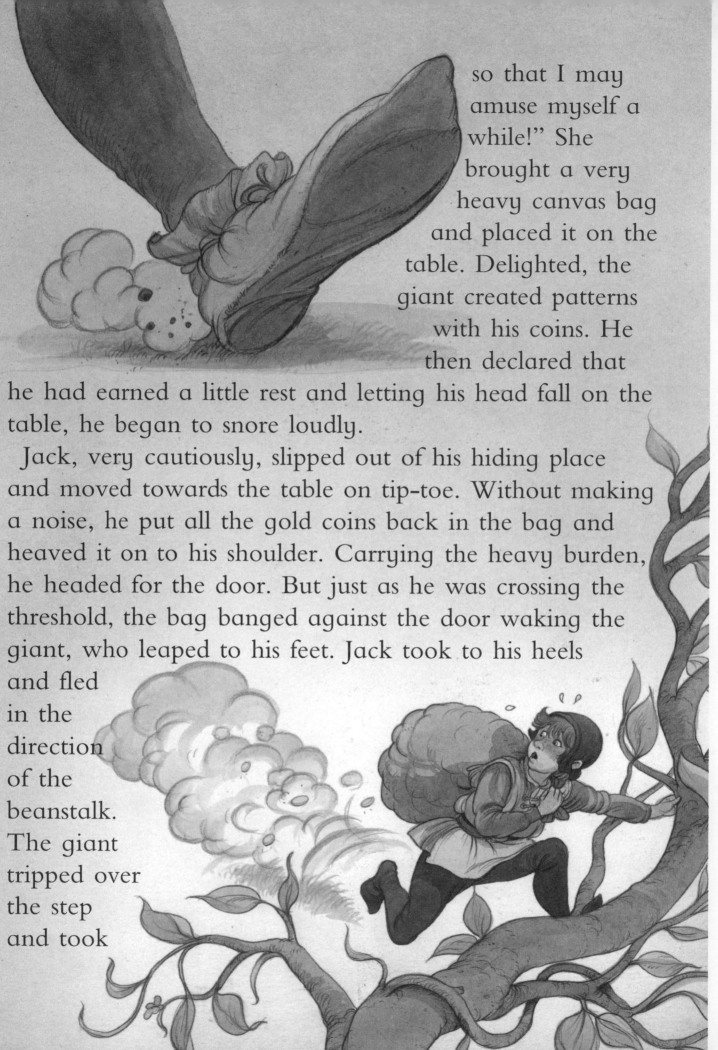

so that I may amuse myself a while!" She brought a very heavy canvas bag and placed it on the table. Delighted, the giant created patterns with his coins. He then declared that he had earned a little rest and letting his head fall on the table, he began to snore loudly.

Jack, very cautiously, slipped out of his hiding place and moved towards the table on tip-toe. Without making a noise, he put all the gold coins back in the bag and heaved it on to his shoulder. Carrying the heavy burden, he headed for the door. But just as he was crossing the threshold, the bag banged against the door waking the giant, who leaped to his feet. Jack took to his heels and fled in the direction of the beanstalk. The giant tripped over the step and took